FACELESS MONSTERS

The ATLANTIS Collective

ORIGINAL WRITING

© 2010 THE ATLANTIS COLLECTIVE

All rights reserved. No part of this publication may be reproduced in any form or by any means—graphic, electronic or mechanical, including photocopying, recording, taping or information storage and retrieval systems—without the prior written permission of the authors.

ISBN: 978-1-907179-69-3

A CIP catalogue for this book is available from the National Library.

Published by ORIGINAL WRITING LTD., Dublin, 2010.
Printed by CAHILLS PRINTERS LIMITED.

Acknowledgements

The Atlantis Collective would like to thank the following

Páraic, Vicki and all at Galway Arts Centre

Maureen Kennelly and everyone at Cúirt

John Kenny, Adrian Frazier, Dearbhla Mooney and all involved with the MA Writing at NUI Galway

Kevin, Simon, Mark, Ken and the crew at Massimo

Dermot Healy, Des Kenny, Vinny Browne, Olaf Tyaransen

Killian Dunne

The Commander's Magic Mouse

David Kelly at Ambient Age, Sarah Quigley, and Jack Harte and everyone at The Irish Writers' Centre

Caroline Gannon and Castle Print

Last, but by no means least, we would like to thank Nuala Ní Chonchúir, for allowing us to borrow recklessly from her wealth of experience.

Contents

Foreword by Nuala Ní Chonchúir 3

Rumpled Quilt Skin by Dara Ó Foghlú 5

Oculoterra by Aideen Henry 11

Dry Land by Máire T. Robinson 21

The Boatman by Alan Caden 29

Row Me Up Some Whiskey, Joe by Paul McMahon 45

Rather Play With Frogs by Trish Holmes 47

Faceless Monsters by Dara Ó Foghlú 59

Haast by Colm Brady 61

Mother America by Nuala Ní Chonchúir 69

Breeding by Conor Montague 75

The Disposable Girl by Máire T. Robinson 93

Ice-Cream Man by Paul McMahon 101

Shapeshifter by Aideen Henry 105

A Monkey Is For Life by Dara Ó Foghlú 117

Wood Chopper by Trish Holmes 133

Carton Press by Paul McMahon 135

María Magdalena by Alan Caden 143

A Shoe Falls by Colm Brady 155

Foreword

If the short story is about obsessions, then the writers in *Faceless Monsters* are obsessed with monkeys and batteries, boats and murder, puppies and broken love. But most of all, like every literary fiction writer, they are obsessed with teasing out the whys and wherefores of the human condition: Why do we love? How many ways can we be cruel to one another? Will life always be this lonely and confusing?

Having met the members of the Atlantis Collective at a day-long workshop, I was delighted when they asked me to edit their (now) annual anthology. I knew them for a committed, hard-working, enthusiastic and light-hearted group of writers. They are truly a collective in that the group works incredibly well together and their ethos is one of improvement and learning. Each writer draws from a separate well – there are the humorists and the dark-lovers, the long-short writers and the flash aficionados – but they are all clearly dedicated to achieving excellence in their art.

The short story is an intense form – when done well, it opens quickly, drags the reader inside and doesn't let her out again until she is satisfied. The stories here achieve all of that. Each one is also its own realised world, full of sparky language and delicious moments. Stories tend to revel in the unpredictable and they often contain something surprising – the writers featured here are not afraid of the odd, the unconventional and the plain weird.

A story needs to resonate emotionally with the reader and, ideally, will have the power to smack her with its truthfulness. Flannery O'Connor said that short fiction should be 'short but deep' – she meant, I think, that the human condition must be illuminated in some way. Short stories are short, yes, but they are also profound and can make a deep impact. The absurdities of all human life are thoroughly explored in this book; the writers here say a lot – and say it well – in a handful of pages.

I love to see flash fiction in a submissions pile. Flash stories are often daring and can bear re-reading over and over. Their writers value brevity of expression as much as any poet. Flash is one of those pure forms – these type of stories are told with an almost absurd economy but they still manage to offer enormous reading pleasure.

Writing is, by its nature, a solitary act. Whether a writer writes full- or part-time, they do it on their own. Writers' groups are there for feedback on the work, but the actual writing will take place with only the writer and the blank page. It strikes me that the writers in the Atlantis Collective have found a happy balance between the cloistered and the communal – they get the writing done; they come together to make it better, and then they share it with readers.

Nuala Ní Chonchúir, Editor.

Galway, March 2010

Rumpled Quilt Skin

By Dara Ó Foghlú

The girl is still asleep. I sit up in bed and look down at the pink mound of rumpled quilt. Her face is visible through a small crack between the covers and pillows. She is sporting a mulberry shiner, and blood has welled up to fill a gash across the bridge of her nose. Her mouth is twisted down and smudged with lipstick. I put my finger under her nostrils. She isn't breathing.

The word 'murder' knocks about in my head like a penny in a washing machine, and my future stretches out before me in full-colour sketches. There I am shackled in the dock; the judge in his wig, cracking a gavel; my mother and my father in the gallery looking like they were the ones being sentenced. Then jail and its affiliate dangers: showers and shanks. And that would be it.

'Aw-www,' she says, then, pulling air in through a long deep groan.

Sleep apnoea. I knew about this stuff. I once lived with a fat man who had it as well. When he went to sleep he'd breathe out until there was no oxygen left in his blood, and then, as if he were within touching distance of death, he'd heave in air, the soft palette at the back of his throat reverberating. Every night he sounded like he would die. His girlfriend threatened to leave him regularly.

'I can't sleep beside you anymore,' she was always saying. 'You sound like a zombie, or something.'

I'm glad the girl beside me is still alive. That's something, I suppose. I try to remember her name. But it's no good. My hangover is rapping at a loose window pane somewhere in my head.

We'd met the night before at a graduation ball for acting, publishing, and writing students. She was a publisher's date, I think. But she had ended up with me. Someone let it slip that the function was closing early and everyone ran to the small strip of a bar in the corner of the ballroom. That's where I met her – sandwiched in the queue. All of us making thirsty eyes at the barman.

I said to her, 'If I get served first I'll get both our drinks. How's that?'

'Deal,' she said. 'I'll do the same. What are you drinking?'

'Double Captain and Coke. Be sure he remembers the lime.'

She had an unreasonably plump bosom surrounded by a blinding corona of light. I couldn't focus on anything else.

'Mine's a Double Gin and Tonic, so.' She was saying.

'What's that? I can't hear you.' I put my ear next to her mouth and looked down into the sliver of darkness between her breasts.

'My drink – it's a G and T.'

'Of course, yeah.'

There was no fucking way the barman was going to serve me before her. Not with her chest rolling out in front of her like that.

She paid for our drinks. She *insisted*. I don't know why, it's not like I was putting up a fight. I found a free table near the bar. We sat down and put our drinks on the white table cloth splattered with gravy and red wine. All around us people in tuxedos and shiny gowns were dancing and falling over and throwing their tongues into each other. It was like the end of the world.

We were talking about something, or not talking at all, or kissing, when she said something like,

'I'll be back in a sec,' or maybe, 'I'm going to be sick.'

She kicked off her heels and ran to the Ladies in her stockings.

When she came back she looked sleepy and lop-sided.

'Feeling better?' I said.

'Much,' she said, then slipped on a puddle of spilled beer and smashed her face off the corner of the table. While she was down on all fours, blood came out of her nose in long strings. Then she heaved an island of puy lentils and chewed pork belly onto the polished floorboards. Splashes landed on my shoes and her hands. When she was done she wiped her fingers, and then her face, on the edge of the tablecloth.

'Let's go to another table,' I said.

'Perfect,' she said.

Later on, back at her place, she tugged at me like she wanted to uproot me, like she wanted one of her own. Maybe she'd keep it in a jar on a special shelf along with all the others. I closed my eyes and tried to think of something kinky, but it was no good. I slid down the bed and put my head between her legs, but that was no good either. My tongue came back with the acrid tang of piss. So I kissed her. See how much she liked it.

Her hand made another jolt towards my crotch. I tried to move inside her where she couldn't clutch at me. But it was a no go.

'Not on the first night,' she squeaked, 'I barely know you.'

'Yeah, you're right,' I said. 'It would only ruin things.'

In the morning, I ease out of the bed and find my suit on the floor next to a flouncy blue ball gown flecked and drizzled with blood. She wakes up as I'm putting on my shoes.

'Oh. Morning,' she goes.

'My head,' I say.

'Mmm, me too.'

'I gotta go,' I say. 'I'm dying. Really dying.'

'Call me sometime,' she says, as I'm nearly out the door.

'Yes,' I say.

But what would I even call her?

Oculoterra

by Aideen Henry

Kieran's home is full of traps, things forgotten, like homework and brushing teeth. Having the wrong answers to questions, like 'Do you think I'm an idiot?' or 'You don't really hate your sister, do you?' All the good stuff has hurdles he must clear first.

'Four more weeks of not cursing and Dr Octavius will be mine'. Kieran sticks out his tongue, pulls his lower lids down so they look like his grandfather's bloodshot droopy eyes and in a gravelly voice says, 'You're a grand little fecker. Aren't you?'

He flushes the toilet and lets the tap run as if he is washing his hands. He sniffs his fingers. He needs longer thumbnails for opening knots on his fishing line. Then he pulls the navy towel off the wooden rail and wraps it, scarf-like, around his head. He puts on his mother's no-time-for-any-of-your-crap face, squashes his nose against the mirror and screws up his eyes to make them bulge like two black golf balls.

'You're just like your father, you little bleep, selfish to the bleep, and all I bleeping do for you.'

Kieran's real home is a faintly visible satellite of the moon, best seen on a cold, clear November evening;

Oculoterra is a freckle seen in the white of the eye of the dying moon. There, his mother is a warm bath that never overheats or cools. He steps in and out of her whenever he pleases. He bathes in her while he sleeps. And even when he leaves, he can still smell her like perfume on the inside of his wrists. His father is a talking goalpost. When Kieran scores, his father cheers and tells him how many miles per hour each ball travels and the odds ratio of Gawky Lydon saving it. Kieran's sister is the jittery feeling he gets when jumping off the top diving board or catching his first mackerel on his new three line hook, on a wet summer evening.

He closes the bathroom door behind him, switches off the fan and lip-syncs his mother as she shouts, 'Did you flush and switch off the fan?'

Without answering he runs out the door, the tips of his new football boots gripping the lino. The door slams behind him, shaking in its frame. He slows down as he gets to the green. Jonathan, a fair-haired boy with a cowlick and brown eyes, is driving the go-kart his father made him, with PJ standing on the back. PJ is tall with buck-teeth, a slouch and matchstick legs. Kieran stands on the kerb, chewing the cuff of his sleeve, staring after them and then at his boots. They spin the go-kart in front of him with a handbrake turn making him jump back.

'What's with the gammy boots, Kieran?' Jonathan says.

'Want to play football?'

'Well, PJ', says Jonathan, imitating his voice, 'are we playing football with this retard?'

PJ giggles, his lips uncovering a gummy smile and they speed away, Jonathan shouting back, 'Try the Brazilians, gay boy, they're always up for it.'

Kieran watches them leave the estate and joins Romero and Juan on the next green, relieved they don't speak English, just football.

Mornings in Oculoterra are spent building go-karts from the architect's plans. Each go-kart has a detachable throne with a self-inflating balloon to the rear and pedal steering on the front wheels. He leads the trail of go-karts down the steep burnt-orange tartan track that runs into the purple helium sea. The trick is to pull the chord just before the front wheels hit the gassy water. The go-kart launches into the air suspended from its balloon; he spends hours gliding and tumbling, rolling and sliding in the thick air over Oculo Bay. His balloon is a playful puppy. It refuels by diving into the bubbling bay then blows him out of the water like whale spray. He takes turns to lead and be led in the dance with the balloon. When he tires, the balloon swings around and scoops him up like a giant palm with his hands and feet spilling over the sides. It carries him back to his cushioned pod in the palace where he naps. When he wakes up, a book opens and reads itself to him while his gaze drifts out the window to look at clouds of taffeta. There are no rules so he can pick his nose, curse or hold his willy whenever he pleases. There is no school so no need to plot skirmishes and counter attacks against Patrick O'Toole in the yard. No bruised shins or scratchy lice either.

Kieran sleeps in the box room. If he lies on his bed with his arms overhead, his fingertips can touch one wall while his toes touch the other. His wardrobe door is covered with pictures of Chelsea footballers. Stuck to his mirror are pictures of toy warriors that can be twisted to make cars or tanks. By his bedside is a box of all his scary plastic characters from wrestling, *Batman*, and *Harry Potter*. He just needs Dr Octavius to complete the set. His mother has called him twice for school but he has a few more minutes before the high-pitched screech is due, the one she uses when she really means it.

Just as his face finds a cool part of the pillow to rest on, she surprises him by sitting on his bed. She never comes into his room. She looks around just the way he does when he is at the aquarium, watching turtles stroke the water. Something's up. She's not screaming. She's not in her there-could-be-ten-mammies-in-there dressing-gown. She's wearing her very-important perfume and using her serious conversation voice. Fuck. She starts stroking his face. It must be bad. She starts talking in grown-up duck and dive. She is staring at the duvet, her left eye blinking while her right stays open, looking glazed. He looks over her shoulder at Ronaldinho, pretending to listen, waiting it out. Bet he wouldn't talk and talk like this. Just plays, speaks with his feet. Kieran waits for the meaning. It usually follows after a pause, a deep breath and a 'So …' Here it is.

'So, we have decided that it's best for everyone if your father moves out.'

'He's Dad. Don't call him "your father". Why? What happened anyway?'

'But I've just explained, dear.'

She has that patient look she gives the really thick kids she teaches in her remedial class. Kieran used to sit into her 'special' class when he finished school an hour earlier in Babies. Why do they call them special anyway? They're just thick or not listening. Then he gets a terrible thought and starts crying.

'Ah, now, now. What is it?' she rubs his cheek.

'Does this mean he'll dress like a girl and we'll never see him?'

'Now why would you say that?'

'My friends will think my Dad is a gay.'

The moment of sweet sadness when his mother holds both his cheeks in the palms of her hands and looks deep into his eyes is broken by Sly Susan, his sister, slithering at the door.

'He's getting Tootsie crossed with Mary Poppins. Poor kid.'

His mother laughs, and then checks herself when she sees his face. 'Ah, no, Kieran. You'll see your father every weekend, no problem.'

'So how long is it for anyway?'

His mother and Sly exchange looks. 'It's for the moment. For the time being.'

Sly moves into his room, pulls her hair back, ties it in a ponytail, stands in side view to the mirror admiring her new breasts and high curved bum.

'Out,' Kieran roars. 'Out of my room. Now! I want to get dressed.'

'Well, that's good to hear,' says his mother, standing up. Sly smirks as she slopes out.

In the evenings, after marbles, he goes hunting or fishing. Hunting is great because it is real. He can choose whom he will hunt and they always show up. He carries one spear while two Irish wolfhounds, Fite and Fuaite, carry his spares. The forest is a breathable green liquid he swims through, undulating his body, head first, with his spear at his side. The trees are black seaweed with eel-like leaves and branches moving like hair under water. When he spots his prey he shouts 'Halt'; they freeze. Then he shoots them. The spears pinch as they go through, like needles through silk, then return to his hand until his prey says the magic words, 'Kieran, you are king. I am your humble servant.'

Sometimes they are so thick he has to give them hints. The boys are quicker than the girls. The girls scream at him not to touch them. As if. Once they have said the magic words their pinprick wounds re-seal, they unfreeze and he can go on hunting. Sometimes he hunts the same person all evening. Other times he goes fishing.

This broken-home craic is pretty good; his father does stuff with him on Saturday and Sunday afternoons, like going to football matches and teaching him how to play pool. And his mother rubs him on the head more and on the backs of his shoulders. Her hugs last longer too. Sly has wangled an iPod out of Dad. She just has to sulk and say she's having a bad time at school, Dad's chin puckers and his eyes look up over their heads to the place where the family was before it broke up. Kieran doesn't care as long as Dr Octavius is on the way.

On Saturday afternoon Kieran stands as usual outside HMV. He looks at the beams of white light shining skywards from glass discs in the ground and wonders are they lights coming from an underworld where all is bright and cheerful and where scatters of light escape through its sieve-like roof, into the floor of his grey day. Dad's late. He's smiling too much, leering and slurry too. He smells bad as he presses his lips to Kieran's forehead. Kieran ducks away from him and checks that no one has seen. They go to the big screen in Fitzers and Kieran sips a coke. Dad is scary. He stares at the wall below the screen and doesn't seem to hear Kieran when he tells him he has to go early.

Kieran runs home, not stopping as he usually does to peg stones at the upturned Tesco trolley in the canal. There's a blue BMW in the driveway with a baby seat in the back. In the kitchen there's a big thing sitting in Dad's seat. It's got a wide face, too many teeth, sticky short hair and shiny tanned skin. It's got its hairy paw on his mother's bottom as she stands beside it. His mother jumps when Kieran comes in. The thing starts talking,

'Delighted …wonderful …super!'

Spit flies out of its mouth, landing on Dad's armrest. Kieran watches a ladybird walk over the back of his father's chair. After the thing's paw has mussed his hair, the same paw that was on his mother's bottom, it sits back in Dad's chair again, its mouth still making lots of noises. Kieran's mother makes tea, glancing from Kieran to the thing and back, pretend-smiling. Kieran escapes with a basket of wet laundry out to the clothesline. He grabs his sister's iPod from the key hook on the way out and puts in the earphones.

He stretches the heavy cotton towels taut, overlapping two corners under each peg, while looking in the kitchen window. His mother is jumpier, all girly. He can see Sly in her. Her clothes are different. Kieran gives every pair of sockwoks and briary a peg each. He stretches two cardrigeens over three pegs. His underpunders look lonely so he puts two to a peg. From behind the sheets he spies on the thing again. It's wide, not tall. It has tree trunk legs and swirls of hair on its bare arms, with tufts creeping out over the top of its shirt collar. Maybe it has goat's legs. Kieran wonders what its roar is like.

His mother looks nervous as it paws her again then it takes its covering from the coat hook, sticks its tongue in his mother's mouth and leaves. Kieran stands over the empty basket, his two hands on the washing line holding it below eye level. His Adam's apple moves up and down behind the sheets. He has nothing to swallow. He looks up at the grey sky. Cloud covers it like a crochet skullcap; fluffy holes of blue visible through it here and there. A plangent love song plays in the middle of his head, resounding in the soft flesh of his chest and stomach.

'Fuck. Fuck. Fuck.' he says. He kicks the empty wash basket against the wall, runs inside and upstairs to his bedroom locking the door. He pulls out the earphones and throws himself face down on his bed.

The best place to fish is Lake Gratitude. He uses a line with a hook the size of a clenched fist. There are no fish in the lake but he always catches something. He stands astride the limestone shelf and whips his rod until his line shimmies across to the centre of the lake where it drops deep, making the sound of a coin landing in an empty tin can. He begins to reel it in. Sometimes objects like a leather handbag or a white car surface, other times a fur hat or a velvet couch. Once the object surfaces it looks around for him and rushes to tell its story.

'I belonged to a woman once who ...'

Every story is different but they all have the same pattern; something awful has happened to each of the owners. Once the story is told the object submerges again. Kieran can ask it two questions before it disappears. He always asks the same two. 'What football team did your owner support?' And, 'Did she or he have beautiful hands?' Once the object has answered it disappears completely. Then the sound of a clacking sewing machine fills the air.

Dry Land

by Máire T. Robinson

So this is the apocalypse. No ball of flame to eradicate us, no scuttling away as molten lava spews, no earth ripped open with us flailing towards its burning centre. Just the splish. Just the splash. Just the splish, splash, splish. Of constant rain. The constant sound like the repetition of an irritating child. *But why, why, why? But why?* Bucketing down. Fucketing down. Drown the lot of us and be done with it. Sweep us away and put us out of our misery for good.

You once said it was only a matter of time before the people of Galway evolved to form gills. How else could they survive in this city with forty shades of rain? It falls at impossible angles, foiling the tightest raincoats, weaselling its way down necks, rendering umbrellas useless. It seeps through the soles of shoes, into the soles of feet. It creeps into bones and marrow where it festers causing unshakable colds and dark thoughts and an unquenchable thirst for drinking pints in front of warm fires.

It falls on us now as we walk to the bus station. You offered to walk me. I never asked you to.

'I've to go to the shop anyway.' You shrugged.

We follow the path of the River Walk. There are railings to our right and a drop to the river below. On the other side is the canal and a grassy bank. We stop and look down at the river from our elevated spot. We are already soaked to the skin, so there's no point in hurrying now. It is the type of rain that steals your breath and makes you gulp for air like a fish on land. You lean on the railings, clear your throat, hock up a lump of phlegm and spit it into the river. It gets caught on the wind and flies back towards you.

You step back to avoid it. 'Fuck sake. D'ya see that?'

I shake my head and smile.

We continue on to where the path meets the bridge and the main road. The river surges forward, relentless, angry, brown. The colour of stew gone cold. The colour of unloved shoes. It forms white-foamed waves which crash in on each other from all directions. A heron stands on the bank, its shoulders hunched as though to protect itself from the elements. In the canal, salmon swim against the fast-flowing stream. We watch as they throw themselves in vain at the closed sluice, their bodies making dull thudding sounds before they splash back into the water. Ducks waddle, unperturbed, on the bank of the canal or sit, heads tucked down, in a line like a cosy shooting gallery. The water smashes off the stone at the base of the Salmon Weir Bridge, determined to make it collapse and be swept out to sea, taking the cars with windscreen-wipers squeaking, and pedestrians doing battle with inside-out umbrellas along with it.

'At this rate the whole city will be underwater,' you say.

I think of a picture from primary school. The teacher asked us to draw the house we wanted to live in when we grew up. I sketched a thatched cottage, a thin pencil line of smoke coming from the chimney, a sleepy cat sitting on the window sill.

The teacher leaned over and looked at my effort. 'Isn't that only lovely, Anne? Well done.' She pointed at the expanse of blue surrounding the house. 'And is this the sky?'

'No, that's the sea.'

'The sea?'

'Yes,' I said. 'I want to live in the sea.'

'Oh, so this must be a boat.'

'No, it's a house, you patronising fuck.'

No, I didn't say that. But I should have. They never listened. Any of them. Useless.

We head in to the shop near the bus station.

'Paul picked a good time to get out of here,' you say, wiping rainwater from your face.

'Yeah, I suppose.'

I came to Galway for his going away party. I was only supposed to stay one night. Now somehow it's four days later. There have been a lot of those parties recently. Everyone is going somewhere. Australia, Canada, Argentina. Except you.

Except me. We always said we would but never did. I can't imagine you in a different climate anyway, on some beach wearing flip-flops or trying to stand up on a surfboard. I can't picture you under any sky except this rainy one. I tried to go somewhere myself but only got as far as Dublin. I suppose it's a start. I even got a job.

'I'm through with all of that,' I said.

'All of what?' You asked, but you knew what I meant. Those nights bleeding into one another. Everything blurring into one prolonged shit party of earnest conversations, hugging people you can't stand, dancing for hours to the same song on repeat. And me and you when everything runs out. Waiting for the pub to open. Crawling into some unmade bed together.

'I could use a pint,' you say, giving me that sideways glance. I could use one too, but I pretend not to hear. We've been wearing the same clothes for days. I was supposed to be back at work yesterday. I should have called and made up some excuse. Said I was sick. But it would have made everything real again.

There's no platform for our departing scene. No steam train, like in films, or final whistles or tearful women waving hankies. Just a brightly lit bus station with a vending machine in the corner and a homeless man on the bench. We drip puddles of rain-water onto the floor. You shake yourself like a wet dog.

'When are you down again?'

'Dunno.' I swing the plastic bag in my hand.

'Right, well ...'

'If you're in Dublin ...' I say.

'Nah, I don't think I will be for a while.'

A queue has formed beside the bus. The driver opens the doors and starts to let people on.

'Okay ...well, thanks for coming down.'

You lean forward to kiss me but I turn away.

'I didn't come here to see you. I came down for the party.'

'Yeah, I know,' you say.

'So, what are you saying thanks for?'

A droplet of water falls from your hat and rolls down the bridge of your nose. I follow its path as it traces the tip and drips onto the floor.

'I was just ...I don't know.'

'I better go,' I say.

The bus stinks like a hangover. The window seats are all taken. I scan the faces as I make my way down the aisle, looking for the person who is least likely to strike up a conversation with me. I sit beside a fat man listening to an iPod. We pull out of the bus station onto the main road.

Rain lashes the roof of the bus and the windscreen wipers squeak over the constant rumble of the engine. I close my eyes but know I won't sleep. Shadows pass in the corners of my eyelids. The fat man tears open a packet of crisps. The smell of synthetic cheese and onion wafts over to my nostrils. Two rows ahead, a couple tend to a baby who is never quiet. They take turns passing him to each other. He alternates between roaring cries and gurgling laughter, as though every single thing in his world is either terrifying or hilarious. Never silent. Jesus Christ. How can they stand it? That could have been us. But then it could never have been us.

I consider eating the sandwich I bought in the shop but decide I can't face it. At the thought of it my stomach lurches.

I tap the man beside me on the shoulder. 'Think I'm gonna be sick.'

He gives me a startled look and removes the headphones from his ears.

'Hah?' He says through a mouthful of crisps.

'Gonna be sick. Ya might wanta move.'

I stand in the aisle with my hand clamped over my mouth as he hastens to gather up his possessions and moves into a seat a couple of rows ahead. I sit back down, open the plastic bag and vomit a stream of clear liquid onto the sandwich inside. It sears my throat. I half expect it to burn a hole right through the bag. I take a drink of water but it comes straight back up again. I'm not sure what to do with the bag, so I tie a knot in the top of it and leave it sitting on my lap. Inside, the vomit sloshes to the rhythm of the bus.

At least I have the window seat now that the man is gone. I edge over and look out as we head into Galway County. We pass field after field, all flooded. Cold blue plots divided by low stone walls. Trees protrude from a blanket of rippling water. It seems impossible that these fields will ever be dry again. Nature has been turned on its head and solid ground has been replaced by water. Galway has become Venice. Locals will have to adapt to their new surroundings. Sheep will look on as farmers traverse their land in gondolas. People will look at the flood damage, shake their heads and say that nature is cruel. But it's not. Nature is indifferent to us and to itself. Chaos. Messy and spilling over. You can only try your best to contain it. And now every submerged field I pass carries me further away from you, towards the promise of dry land.

The Boatman

by Alan Caden

Beans and rice, as usual. Perhaps she might add some fish, or if he was really lucky some chicken in spicy sauce. He was starving and exhaustion was in his bones as he came back from the last trip of the day. Almost dusk now. It wasn't normal that he should finish so late. His wife would be worried. And when she was worried, that meant a hard time for him.

It had been a long day and the mantle of the heat was inescapable. It had come down upon the river like thick soup, well before noon, soaking his clothes in sweat and hurting his head even through the old fisherman's hat. He had lost count of how many crossings he had made, back and forth without a break since five-thirty in the morning. Families with crying children, drunken loggers, farmers with chickens that left shit and feathers all over his boat, Indians barely out of the jungle, and many others. Business was good these days. Everybody wanted to cross to the other side of the river because the guerrillas were acting up again to the north. The new road that led to the bridge was not safe. The government had sent troops in, and everyone knew what that meant. The river was the line. Most people were heading for the shanties outside Santa Elena. But Pele wasn't going to move. There had always been fighting around here. It would pass by, as fighting always did. He considered that people always outlive war. Life goes on but things never change. The water changes but the river does not.

Darkness was coming quickly so with one hand firm upon the motor, he used the other to count the money he had made that day. It wasn't much, of course, but if he worked like this every day then maybe in a few months he could buy some pigs. He'd be able to pay Concepción's school-master. Perhaps he could even begin to think about getting a new motor, so he could make more journeys, more money and then think of buying a bigger boat, maybe even one that could take jeeps so people wouldn't have to go as far as the bridge. These were dreams, just dreams. He was too old for them now. He had spent his life on this river, and many others. His dreams were memories of dreams, tributaries that had never reached the sea. He had captained boats ten times the size of this one, up and down the labyrinth of watery highways; the highways that God built, he called them. That was in the days when there were no roads up here, and the river was full of traffic. Now, days could pass without seeing another boat.

He wrapped the heavy rope once around the mooring post and breathed a sigh. He returned to thumbing through the worn and sweaty notes, trying to outpace the plummeting sun. His eye was caught by a water-boatman perched on top of a pool of scummy water in the bottom of the boat. The poor thing skated anxiously from one side of its prison to the other, back and forth, its legs extended out without breaking the surface tension. As Pele reached down to gently pick it between his calloused fingers, he spotted two figures coming down to the bank in the dim light. He stowed the money under his hat. He did not like to be seen counting it like a miser. The taller one hailed him, and spoke using the polite form.

'Hello and good evening to you, sir. Is the barge still going or have we come too late?'

Both of the strangers were young men, dressed in ragged and dirty clothes; the uniform of the poor. They looked lean and thirsty. They were sweating and exhaustion was evident on their faces. They looked as though they had come a long way. The smaller one stood favouring his right leg.

'No, young fellas,' said Pele, 'I'm afraid I've just finished up for the day. It's late and I should be getting home.' He secured the stern to the legs of the jetty and gathered his possessions.

'Please, sir,' said the taller man. He had the light skin and smooth accent of the city. 'We've come a long way today and we've had many delays. We are tired. We have friends waiting for us in the next village and they will be worried if we don't arrive.'

The smaller one, with the wide, inscrutable face of the highlanders, nodded and motioned vaguely to the other side of the river where the only person who lived was Juan José, a bad-minded poacher. Pele would have been surprised to learn he had friends.

'Really, gentlemen, I understand but I'm very sorry. You'll have to wait until the morning. I'll be here at dawn, without fail.'

It sometimes happened that people came late and wanted a last trip across, but the night-time trip was slower and more difficult. Besides, two fares wouldn't even pay for the gasoline. Most would be content to wait until the morning; the jungle people were patient and it was strange for them to have deadlines beyond those of harvest and flood. But he did not recognise these two and they carried no baggage. The refugees are coming from further and further. The shorter one looked to be close to collapsing and was being supported by his taller companion. On his leg was a filthy bandage through which a tint of reddish-brown could be seen. He was staring wordlessly at Pele's water-bottle, which hung on his shoulder.

'Ah, you must be thirsty. Drink. I have more at home,' said Pele once the silence had become uncomfortable. He took the water and gave it to the darker one. He gulped deeply and then passed it to his friend, who put down a machete in order to take a long drink. He let out a satisfied sigh and then turned to study Pele.

'Well, if we can't cross we'll need somewhere to stay the night. Perhaps we could accompany you, sleep on the ground if that's okay. That way, we'll be ready at the same time in the morning.' He was well-spoken and his almond-shaped eyes held Pele's gaze in the fading light.

'I'm not sure if there's enough room,' said Pele, 'but I think there are places to stay in the last village you passed.'

Passengers had stayed with him before, but he did not want two young strangers staying in his house, especially now his granddaughter was of the age to attract attention. These were men desperate to cross the river and he did not want desperate men in his shack.

'But the last village is kilometres away,' said the dark one. 'We'd never find it in the dark.'

'The river is wide, my friends, and dangerous to cross at night. Could you not sleep here and wait until the morning? There is, after all, a curfew.'

'No,' said the tall one. 'We have to go now. My friend is not well, and we cannot wait to be bitten alive by mosquitoes here. We'll pay you extra, or double if you like. Please, sir.'

Pele thought on this. The men were adamant. If he didn't take them across, then they would be wandering around all night. They might follow him to his house. He always tried to see the best in people, to attribute noble motives and intentions to them, but he knew that poverty can overcome this. He did not fear them, but he feared for his family. His wife said he was getting too old. His dinner would be getting cold, but he could heat that up when he got back. Concepción would probably still be up by the time he returned. His stomach groaned, feeling the decision had already been made. Maybe it was best just to take them across and have done with it. He could be back in an hour.

'If you insist, my friends. You really are in a hurry to get across, aren't you? Anyway, I have one price and that's it – I charge everyone the same. It'll be five each, please, and I'll ask you to pay first. I'm sorry, but that's just the way I do it.'

Important to let them know from the start that he was in charge, and that it was business as normal. He knew well there were many bandits in these parts, and rebels too, but that didn't worry him, he had been a tough man in his day in the bars and docks of the river ports and had the scars to prove it.

'Thank you, sir. Thank you so much,' the tall one said, while the dark one looked to his companion with an unspoken question.

'Yes. Pay the man,' he ordered, and the dark one dug in his jacket. He produced a crumpled, torn ten and gave it to Pele.

Now that he had decided to go, Pele went into work mode with no complaints or reluctance. He readied the boat for the crossing, pouring a little more gasoline into the motor.

When people asked him if he ever got sick of the repeated crossings day after day, he told them he didn't. Each crossing, the cargo or the people were different, or the level of the river was slightly higher or lower than usual. Sometimes the currents changed, sometimes they were stronger. There might be a wind, there might not. Most of the time there were pieces of driftwood, or other bits of flotsam on the brown water, sometimes from hundreds of kilometres away. So one always had to be careful, especially at night when the only guide was the small light in the prow of the boat. As there were no lights on either bank, it was only instinct that would guide Pele in the dark. Without a good knowledge of the trinity of boat, river and jungle, a man could easily get pulled away by the current. With Pele at the tiller, though, the men would be safe on the passage.

'All right, young men, let's go!' said Pele, trying to sound cheerful and enthusiastic although he was as tired as a sloth. He pushed off the boat, receiving no help from the two men, who sat quiet and satisfied, watching the old boatman carefully. Pele turned the barge around, working the tiller at an acute angle to point the boat the right way. Peque-peque-peque went the motor, frothing up the brown water.

No one said anything for a time as the boat chugged along in the dark. There wasn't silence, for the jungle was never a silent place. Even less so at night. The capuchin monkeys chattered in the trees. In the distance, a howler monkey bellowed his control of the troupe. The plaintive call of the jacaranda advertised for a mate. And behind it all, the overwhelming sound of the crickets, the beetles and the toads. The sounds faded slightly as they moved out diagonal with the current. Eventually, the dark one spoke.

'So this is good work, is it, old man?' His tone was nonchalant, almost disrespectful. Pele thought for a second. 'I suppose it is. I don't mind it, anyway. I've lived my life on the river. She's my only mistress.' He laughed.

'No, I mean …' the man began, but the taller one silenced him with a harsh look.

'So,' said Pele, beginning to feel uncomfortable, 'are you two gentlemen visiting friends on the other side or just getting away from the troubles like all the others?'

'Visiting friends,' said the tall one firmly, 'but after that we'll be pushing on to the east.'

'To the east, eh? You'd want to watch out, there's only logging camps and narco-traffickers over there. It's beautiful, though. I remember – in '72, I think – I captained a lovely boat up those rivers, the *Camila* she was called; two paddles, fifteen crew, a hundred passengers. One time …'

'We'll find out all about it, thanks,' the tall one said, cutting Pele's reminiscences short. The three fell silent again.

The sound of the motor dominated the boat. It was a beast of a thing, a Yamaha that Pele had bought off a *negro* in Santa Elena. It was old and big, but he managed to keep it in shape and he knew the best ways to run it on the least amount of fuel. It needed a lot of maintenance and guzzled a lot of fuel – like his wife, he would joke – but it was reliable and familiar. Some day he might buy a new one, but to tell the truth he was kind of attached to this one, old and tough like himself.

'What are your names, lads?' Pele asked, adopting a friendly tone. If he was doing a favour for them, he thought, the least they could do was give him some conversation to shorten the trip. That was the unwritten rule.

'I'm Loro,' said the darker one instantly, 'and this is Daniel.'

Daniel gave him a quick look of reproof. Pele introduced himself, and shook their hands. He used his real name, Lucio, and not the nickname his Brazilian crew (mostly dead now) had given him. It was because of the darkness of his skin, and nothing to do with any gift for football. He offered them a hand-rolled cigarette of black tobacco, calling them by name, and they accepted. They smoked nervously, and at one point the tall one almost jumped out of his skin when a caiman splashed in the water beside them. Pele laughed and turned the weak light towards the water, where pairs of red eyes gleamed impassively at them. The night was their time. They were calm creatures, whose lazy lives were punctuated by brief bursts of savage energy. Pele smoked his cigarette slowly, allowing it to go out from time to time, savouring that beautiful repose that descended on him when he was on the river. He could feel it all around him, his kingdom, his element. He loved to smoke and think, his hand on the tiller. He only smoked one or two a day, sometimes none, and never at home because his wife and granddaughter would kill him if they caught him.

'Were you busy today, old man?' asked Daniel, straining his voice over the noise of the motor.

'Very busy,' said Pele, and blew out an exhausted sigh. 'Yes, a lot of people today – I suppose the troubles are good for some.'

'I suppose so ...' said Daniel, but he didn't finish his thought. His eyes were attracted by lights back on the bank they had just come from.

'You see, you two weren't even the last!' Pele let out a surprised chuckle. There were torches moving back and forth along the bank in the distance, quite a few of them. This was very strange, but these were strange times. Anyone who knew the jungle knew that it was no place for humans after dark. There were jaguars out there, and other things that hunted in the dark.

Loro and Daniel looked at each other and then back at the bank, but said nothing. Muffled shouts reached them. There were quite a few flashlights as well, strong ones, but not strong enough to illuminate Pele's small boat and his two passengers. Of course, they would be easily able to see the small, naked lamp that swayed above Daniel's head, swinging his face in and out of shadow. Pele was beginning to wonder. He was not naturally nosy, and tended to leave people's business to themselves, but he wanted to satisfy his curiosity about these two. He found that people were normally happy to talk away about themselves. Something about silence that so many people didn't like.

'So where are you two coming from? Was it the soldiers or the guerrillas who drove you out?'

'None of your business,' snapped Loro.

'Excuse me, I was just being curious …or maybe nosy.'

After a short pause, Daniel asked, 'How much further now?'

'We're nearly halfway there,' said Pele, feeling a bit hurt and keeping it brief. He noticed that Daniel kept his hand constantly on his machete.

'So how much would you make in a day, then? In a busy day like today, for example?'

'Oh, not much at all,' said Pele, picking his words. 'Depends on the people. I usually leave most of it back at the other side ...for safety, you know?'

'Now why would he say that to us?' Said Daniel to his comrade with mock wonder.

Loro's gaze was set on the lights on the bank they had come from. The people seemed to be wandering up and down the bank to each side of the jetty. He turned back to Daniel and smiled, joining in on the game.

'Maybe he thinks we're thieves or something?'

'Us?' Daniel snorted, his palms upwards, beseeching God for the patience to endure such implications.

Pele looked back towards the bank, and the lights breaking off into smaller groups that moved up and down either side of the jetty. Whether they were soldiers, guerrillas or war vultures, he didn't know and it didn't matter. All that existed now was the river, the boat and the three of them. To think of his wife and granddaughter now was dangerous. West bank to east. Back again, then home and safe. There was as much hope of help from whoever was searching the bank as there was of the *bufeos*, the pink dolphins, coming to save him.

'Alright, old man, just keep going. Nice and quickly and we'll get to the other side safe and sound,' said Daniel, sensing that something was amiss with Pele.

Pele's heart was thumping and he began to sweat profusely, though the night and the breeze in the middle of the river usually brought a respite from the heavy heat. He thought of all the things that he could try, and he knew none of them would work. In his own boat, on his own river, in his own jungle he was not master – how could this be? He couldn't go like this. He had survived brawls in Manaos, attacks by Indians, jail in Brazil, horrific accidents. Yet he could think of nothing he could do now.

Loro smiled at him, all narrow malice. 'How much would one of those engines cost? How much would you sell one for in Manaos?' Pele's eyes fell on the motor, which he still gripped with his hand. He said nothing.

'Stupid Indian! What are you thinking? Are you going to carry it yourself?' Daniel asked Loro, laughing. Loro's smile vanished. They looked at each other, making themselves ready. Pele spoke first.

'Right, my friends, let's get down to it. I'm not a fool. What do you want?'

Daniel held up the machete in one hand and he turned his other palm upwards.

'What?' asked Pele, buying time to think, perhaps to act.

'You know …'

These parasites. How dare they come here, into his jungle, and onto his boat to tell him what to do. He had worked more in his life than a thousand of these scum, yet it was so simple for them to come and just take what he had earned. Soldiers, guerrillas, politicians, it didn't matter. This country, the Amazon, the hard workers are only prey, snapped up by lazy predators, he thought. Pele was a fair man, a steady, simple hand on the tiller, but sometimes, very rarely, he was more stubborn than the current itself.

'Come on now, Grandad,' Daniel said, 'the money you were counting earlier. Don't be a fool. We've come a long way. Look at us. We need this money. We need it.'

Now it was spelled out, the panic dissipated. A mist had gathered on the river. He didn't regret the decision to take them across, because if he hadn't they would have been wandering near to his house, his wife and his granddaughter. They were going to rob him, beat him, perhaps even kill him, and all he felt was a cold anger. Be wary of those who are slow to anger, his wife always said to him. Those are the most dangerous.

He handed over the wallet from under his hat, his fingers trembling. Loro opened it quickly. The cocky sneer drained from his face. He glanced at Daniel and then rifled through the wallet again.

'Is this it, you black bastard? This is all you make on a busy day? There must be more! Where is it, Granddad? *Where?*'

While Pele paused, not knowing what to do, Loro leaned forward and punched him full in the face, smashing his nose in and knocking him against the gunwale. His hand slipped on the engine and the boat swerved around. He fell onto the floor. Daniel laughed.

Pele looked for the water-boatman but couldn't see it. He took a bloody breath and spat out splinters off tooth.

'Okay, there's more. It's down here beside the motor. I'm sorry, just let me get it for you,' he said, putting one palm up to pacify them.

He leaned down to look for the money while Loro counted what was in the wallet. Daniel stood over him with the machete. With deft fingers that belied their gnarled appearance, Pele loosened the screws. He had already begun this before the men arrived. Too late Daniel realised what Pele was rooting at, and jumped to pull him away. Pele pushed him away with the thick-muscled arms of a sailor, and then pulled the motor up with a mighty heave. Up and over the side it went, and sank down into the musky brown with an anticlimactic gurgle. A caiman thrashed, not knowing what to make of this strange intruder in its river.

Daniel stared. He wobbled a little, then regained his balance and raised the machete. There was no sound but that of the jungle, a thin black silhouette mocking them from both sides. An almost imperceptible ripple told of the direction of the current on the side of the boat, a current that could be said to run all the way to the mouth of the Amazon. Promptly the boat began to turn. It slowed and changed direction. The heat grew as the breeze lessened. The machete did not fall. No-one said a word. They knew they were helpless now, at the river's mercy, and the boatman's.

Pele smiled up at them and spat blood into the river.

'What now, my friends?' he asked.

Row Me Up Some Whiskey, Joe

by Paul McMahon

I didn't mean to kill him, Joe. We were drinking all day. We were living in that one room for three months after you left. It was the end of a long winter. There were five sausages. Who was getting three and who was getting two? I whacked him over the head with the frying pan and ate all five of them, then called the cops. I had every intention of handing myself in until I heard the sirens whirling out on the street, ice-blue flashing through the window. I bolted down the fire-escape and headed for the hills. I used one of our canoes to get up-river. I'm in the cabin we use when we're fishing. I gave this letter to a trapper rowing down river. He gave me his word.

I was at our name-tree today. Birds must have pecked his name off. It's gone. It's lonesome up here, Joe. At night there is no moon; it must be hiding out, like me, behind a sky full of twinkling bullet holes. Is he with the shades on the spectral wastes, drifting through endless day? I hear him screaming with the boiling kettle. When the train rumbles by, it's like I feel him nearing.

I saw the wild horse today, running through the wintered trees – it felt like my youth that was running, scattering my clay-pigeon dreams. Nothing gets through the eye of the needle, Joe. When I look out the window of the shack, it looks like the outskirts of my own brain, the slum-end of my mind. I went roving last night. The sky spun around my head like a prostitute's skirt and the stars flashed like lice and flitted around a swollen gonorrhoea moon.

Everything is hypnotised by the whim, Joe. There is no control; man is a machine droning along like a fly in the wind. If you come, Joe, bring whiskey. Please, Joe, row me up some whiskey, Joe.

Rather Play with Frogs

by Trish Holmes

Curiosity, not theft, is in the forefront of Mary's mind as she tiptoes into her brother's bedroom. Pete Townsend smashes his guitar on one wall. Directly opposite, Farrah Fawcett-Majors poses in a little red number with her hair feathered back. Mary opens the top drawer of her brother's dresser; nothing interesting, only socks. A pile of magazines sticks out from under the bed. She kneels down and pulls them out. Two *Playboys*, a *Hustler*, and three *Penthouses*.

The two women holding each other's breasts on the cover of the first *Penthouse* are far bolder inside. When Mary turns the page to find them licking each other's bums, she shoves the magazines back under the bed and races down the stairs to the kitchen where her mother is flipping through the pages of the *Toronto Star*.

'What are you up to Mary?'

Her mother takes a drag from her cigarette before returning it to the ashtray that sits on a stack of newspapers in the middle of the table. At dinner, they're thrown onto the top of the fridge or into the hutch inherited from her grandparents in Milverton – wherever there was room.

'You want something to drink? Sit down.' Her mother grabs a glass from the cupboard.

'Why does Kevin like Farrah Fawcett-Majors?'

'Why do you think?'

'Because she's in *Charlie's Angels* and she's the best fighter?' Mary pours orange juice into her glass. 'Well, she's pretty. Jennifer is always trying to copy her hair.'

'You're getting warmer. Keep trying.'

'Is it because she wears bikinis all the time?'

'That show off her...'

'Boobs?'

'There you go.' She flicks the growing ash off the end of the cigarette.

'And because she sits like this?' Mary twists to the side and pushes her chest forward, posing with her hands on the back of her head.

'That's it sweetie,' Her mother sips her coffee. 'You got it. You see, when it comes to women, men are interested in two things: looks or money. And you don't need both. Lots of one will do just fine. Take your cousin Kathy, she can thank her lucky stars her father is loaded because that's the only way she's going to get her hooves on a man.'

'Kathy has a boyfriend?'

Her mother nods. 'Exactly.' She wipes the corners of her mouth with her thumb and finger. 'We might not have any money sweetie, but you're lucky, you look like me. Jennifer, she has your father's build, I can see it already, but at least she has my eyes. All my children are beautiful, thank Christ.' She glides her hand through her short hair. 'Listen, you need less time around that bloody frog pond and more time learning the facts of life.'

Mary wonders how her new frog is doing. Yesterday she and her father counted twenty-six frogs in total over at the pond. Some of them were green with a red patch on the back and the others were just brown. The new frog was brown with two patches of red.

'You won't make the same mistake I made, Mary. You'll find a wonderful man. He'll be rich and you'll live in a nice house in the city.'

Mary pushes her long hair behind her shoulders. 'What if he's not rich?'

'Listen, it's the people with money who'll tell you money doesn't matter. But if you don't have it, it's pretty goddamn important. It's just as easy to fall in love with a rich man as a poor man. I wish someone had said that to me – just look at me now in the middle of god-knows-where, living in a dump, and farming bloody pigs. Mary, you're going to live in the city, in Toronto, where people like us should be.'

Mary rests her elbow on the table and her head on her hand.

'You have to be clever about these things. Constantly flatter them, tell them they're clever and funny. But don't show them you're smarter than they are. Nobody gives a damn if you're smart or not. That Watson girl, that's her problem. She can bring them in all right, but they don't come back because she's doesn't know when to shut the hell up.'

If she leaves now she'll make it to the pond before sunset and still have time to bike to the stream, where the day before she'd counted fifteen crayfish.

'Men think it's a kind of victory being with a good-looking woman. Now take your sister, sure, she needs to lose weight, but at least she dresses up and takes the time to do her hair and put on some makeup. That's why boys call on her all the time.'

When her sister is out, Mary often sneaks into her room. In the closet, clothes of a similar colour are hung together, and her makeup on the dresser is organised by the part of the face it's for. Beside the Bonne Bell mascara are two new Max Factor eye shadows she bought at Zellers last week. Apple Daze is the best although Disco Blue is pretty good too. The record collection is in alphabetical order. Mary plucks out the *Blondes Have More Fun* LP and places it on the record player. She drops the needle at the third wide groove on the record and then positions herself in front of the mirror.

Her whole school is here. Now that she's won all those Grammys, they've all come to see her homecoming concert. Never before has one artist won so many awards.

'She sits alone waiting for suggestions,

He's so nervous avoiding all her questions.'

The concert is a gift to her school now that she's hit the big-time. Later, she has to fly back to London on the Concorde because she's singing with The Beatles on their reunion album.

'If you really need me just reach out and touch me,

Come on, honey, tell me so.'

Beautiful Make-Up, *Becoming a Woman*, and a bunch of astrology books sit in order of size on her sister's bookshelf. In *Becoming a Woman*, Mary finds walking exercises to ensure an hourglass figure and on page eighty-four Mary discovers the secret to big breasts. You have to lick them. This, the author points out, stimulates growth. Mary removes her shirt, checks the nipples on her flat chest, reaches her head down, and sticks out her tongue as far down as she can reach. The book recommends a six-month programme. If she starts now she'll be gigantic, bigger than even Farrah.

When everyone is out of the house, she goes to the living room and pushes her father's yellow recliner out of the way. She begins a daily routine of walking exercises: right foot forward with the left hip pushed out to the side, then the other foot forward and the other hip pushed out. At first, the swagger is difficult. She focuses on the bookcase beside the window. She can't corner quite yet, but after a few practice rounds she hits her stride as she tacks past the TV.

Mary still reads her brother's magazines, but now she skips over the bum lickers and instead reads about the frisky hitchhiker, the willing stewardess, and the raunchy librarian. They're surrounded by men and have loads of money. Peggy skinny-dips in her pool and sips Singapore Slings; Cynthia sleeps in the nip on a heart-shaped bed; Janice rides naked on her horse through the woods. Favourite colours: blue, red, pink. Favourite animals: puppies, kittens, horses. Most exciting memory: sex with the school principal; sex with the pilot; sex with the horse whisperer. Future ambition: actress, astronaut, teacher.

Mary says nothing of this to anyone, not even to the girls at school. Most of her friends live in suburbs such as Ferndale Downs or Crossglen Arbours, where young trees line wide streets. Bedtimes and curfews are strictly imposed. Their fathers wear ties to work, their mothers think smoking is disgusting, and their older brothers are too young to buy the kind of magazines Mary's brother does.

Mary usually hangs out beside the gym door with these girls, but today she's watching the basketball game. Dawn Thurston is the only girl playing and she's better than any of the boys, even Stevie Keating. Her team is winning six nothing.

'Think fast, Scary.' Dawn thrusts the ball towards Mary, quick and hard. Mary turns her body, her shoulders fly up towards her ears, and she brings her arms into her chest. The ball bounces off her arm.

'Nice move, Scary. Who taught you to catch a basketball?'

Mary rubs the spot on her arm where the ball hit her.

Dawn stands in front of her. The sun is bright and, according to her sister's book, squinting causes crow's feet, so Mary stares at the ground instead. Dawn's Reeboks move closer.

'You know, Scary,' Dawn grips the orange basketball in her hands. 'You're pretty.' She leans forward. 'Pretty ugly.'

The kid beside Mary giggles. Dawn bounces the ball in front of Mary a few times before she laughs as well. Mary is still staring at the grey tarmac, one hand is on her chest, and the other has stopped rubbing her arm.

'Take your hands down, Scary, you've nothing to protect anyway.' Dawn pretends to throw the ball at Mary, but instead spins back onto the court, manoeuvres around the other players, and then sinks the ball into the basket. Some kids clap.

Mary walks through the crowd and goes into the school. Compared to outside, the corridor is dark. She stops in front of a display cabinet full of trophies and plaques. She sees her reflection in the glass. A band of dark brown freckles stretch out across her nose and, underneath, an ugly mole squats on her cheek. More clapping in the distance. The tap-tap of shoes veers around the corner and then stops behind her.

'What're you doing, Mary?' Sister Teresa asks.

'I fell. I'm okay'

'You don't look okay.'

The nun is going nowhere without an explanation. 'I fell on my elbow, it hurt before, but it's OK now.'

'Let me see.' Sister Teresa grabs Mary's arm, pushes her sleeve up, and inspects her elbow.

'I don't see anything wrong.' The lunch bell rings and the charge of children entering the school bellows through the building. 'Come with me.'

Mary follows Sister Teresa to her office and then sits in a red chair in front of the desk.

'I'll ask you again. What happened?'

She studies the bevelled edge of the desk. Mary shrugs. 'I wasn't...' She touches the little steps of the desk-edge with her fingernail, 'chosen to play on one of the basketball teams.'

'I didn't realise basketball was that important to you.'

On the wall is a painting of a robin redbreast guarding four eggs in its nest. 'Yeah, it is.'

Sometimes if she looked way up into her eyelids she could stop tears. But that doesn't work this time and tears are streaming down her face. Sister Teresa hands her a tissue from the yellow box beside the phone.

'There's always next time.' She waits to speak again until Mary is finished crying. 'You would do well to put less emphasis on other people's opinion of your basketball ability and more on your schoolwork. Do you understand?'

Mary nods.

'Mary, do you understand?' The nun crosses her arms over her chest.

'Yes, Sister, I understand.' Mary thinks about the tiny pink birds tucked tight into their shells, warm and protected from the outside world. Their little beating hearts visible and their eyes still sealed.

The nun checks her watch. 'I have to go, but do not return to class with your eyes like that Mary. When you're ready, go to the bathroom, and put a cold wet paper towel on your eyes so the redness goes away all right? And, Mary, when I ask you what is wrong I expect you to tell the truth. Do you understand?'

'Yes Sister.'

Sister Teresa grabs a cluster of keys off the desk. She leaves the room and closes the door behind her.

The dog runs to meet Mary as she gets off her school bus. She rubs his back and kisses his forehead. He walks with her up the lane to the house, and as she opens the kitchen door he squeezes inside before her. Her mother is at the sink preparing dinner.

'You're home.' Her mother glances over her shoulder.

Mary throws her schoolbag down beside the fridge and searches the counter for any remaining bits of last night's pie.

'Your father had it at lunch.'

Mary groans and goes for a glass of milk instead.

'The bloody phone bill came today.'

She phoned Natalie Garvey last week, but that was only a local call. It was the Toronto phone-calls again. Mary realises now her mother had been crying.

'Goddamned miserable bastard is what he is, Mary. What am I supposed to do – never talk to my family and just have him for company? I don't bloody well think so. Him and his goddamned books. Over my dead body.' She tosses the last potato into a pot. 'Don't worry, I have a bit of money Uncle John gave me. We'll go to Toronto this weekend and get away from the old devil for a few days.' She moves the pot onto the stovetop.

Mary considers not being around at dinner. There is sure to be a fight, but she'd be too hungry and get in more trouble later.

'I'll pick you and your brother up from school on Friday and we'll go straight from there. Don't say anything to him whatever you do. Let him worry. Let him rot.' Her mother dries her hands on the dishtowel and stares at Mary. 'How was school?'

Mary thinks about the robin redbreast and the eggs

on Sister Teresa's wall. After the nun left, Mary climbed up onto to a chair to see the picture close up. The four eggs were bright blue with tiny speckles across them. The robin was looking into the distance; the background was all white except for the tree trunk.

'OK.'

They'd stay at her Uncle John's house and spend a day walking around the shops at the Scarborough Town Centre and later eat at Swiss Chalet or Harvey's. They'd visit Aunt Edna. Mary and her brother would compete to see who could best time the countdown from ten as they drove past the 'Welcome to Metropolitan Toronto' sign on the 401. Mary's favourite thing of all was at the top of the hill on the way to her Uncle's house. Right before the Golden Mile shopping mall was the pretty girl in the red bikini, rocking back and forth on a swing. High up and all alone on a billboard every day and in all kinds of weather advertising a used car dealership somewhere out in the suburbs.

Faceless Monsters

by Dara Ó Foghlú

My girlfriend had been in bed for two days, curled up on her side. I figured something must have gone wrong inside her to make her coil up that way, murmuring and clutching the sheets.

I was in the other room shooting decorations off the Christmas tree with a BB gun. I hit the angel first, her mouth wide open like a shock-faced sex doll. She tumbled from the tip of the tree, screaming O all the way down. Then I picked off the red and white baubles. The bullets pinged through the plastic shell, punching first in and then out the back in bigger exit wounds. Every so often, my stomach lurched like it wanted to walk out on me.

I found a list of resolutions on the coffee table. At some point during the celebrations we must have lost our moorings and decided to write it. I sat on the couch, pistol in one hand and list in the other. A foreign scrawl stumbled down the page, illegible as a doctor's script in parts, then found its balance again in stark bold capitals. Words like 'GYM' and 'VEGETABLES' were bandied about like the basic elements of a magic spell. And there at the bottom, notarised by both our signatures were the words, 'GIVE IT UP'.

In the bedroom, my girlfriend was moaning, being chased through her dreams by faceless monsters. I went outside to leave her fight them alone. When I walked down the street I could hear the dry calcium rasp of my knees. It was freezing, and some guy with his arm in a sling was shuffling along, dragging his shoes over glassy patches of ice. He was looking down at the concrete like you'd look at someone pointing a gun at you. Then he slipped and used his one good hand to break his fall. He stayed down, staring at the white stick of bone coming out of his wrist. His mouth was clamped at the teeth, thick huffs of breath curling out of him. He was probably thinking how his next fall would break his face, or wondering how to wipe his hole now with two busted hands.

I helped him onto his feet and lifted the wallet from his back pocket. When I got home, the apartment had been cleaned and my girlfriend stood in the middle of the room looking like she hadn't meant to do any of this, and didn't know how the yellow rubber gloves got on her hands.

The list was gone. She probably burned it. I came in and kissed her and showed her the few grams I had scored for us.

'Happy New Year, baby,' I said.

'Yeah,' she said, looking at the foil package in my hand, 'I love you too.'

Haast

by Colm Brady

They had been on the road about an hour when the landscape changed. It moved as they drove from scrubby land lit by a wan sun, to rock, scree and shale. The light left shadows behind every grain of sand as the low sun tried to illuminate the blasted vista. The car stuttered and Fishboy awoke on the baby seat. He looked over and his pale eyes took in the car. He wore no expression.

'You are one furry freak,' Haast muttered, and was interrupted by another heave from the engine. The rattle of a blown piston lasted seconds then the cam locked in place, bringing the car to a shuddering halt. The man he bought it off called it the Dead Man's Carry and it looked like it had breathed its last.

He pulled the rucksack from the back and rigged up a sling for Fishboy from some spare webbing; he seemed happy enough to sit in it and supervise. His hands were outstretched reaching for the world as if to embrace it. The back of his neck had a square artificial welt around the chip. It was couched between the layers of flesh and the lettering between the pins was still visible through the translucent skin. The swelling had gone down in the few hours since they left, but Haast still grimaced as he thought of the mechanical snick as he removed the lead from the device in the facility. The fact that the Fishwife had left him there to be probed and calibrated at ten months did not surprise him. In the short time he had known her she had only shown interest in the good times. He could not see her in the maternal role – her mouth had too many corners. Her eyes gave it away. The kid's eyes were not from her, they were too open and hungry for light.

He tramped on through silence that overpowered him and killed the sound of his boots. The fine dust on the margins of the road filled the grooves in the soles and fell free, leaving a little impression with each step. Down here you hitch early in the morning, as lifts are few and you don't want to be out in the freeze. He could practically feel the rocks contract as they worked on creating one more grain of sand for the piles that slipped down the slopes.

Haast realised that this chain of events was only twenty months long. He met her in a pub where there were no seats and you bought Speights by the plastic crate. The affair was brutal and brief and he only heard about Fishboy from a social worker who had come to the hostel two weeks before. She was a florid woman who spoke in careful language about drugs that strip the humanity until all that is left are the bleached bones. Fishboy was sometimes fed and sometimes not. He was wise enough to know that crying would not improve things. He had only been in Haast's company for a day but he seemed content; maybe he would have accepted anyone that could deliver him from the cruel instruments.

'Right wee man, we have to get out of here before dark. The heater in the car is dead so there will be no second chances.'

They waited.

Just as the sun dropped, they heard the roar of a poorly-tuned exhaust. It was a Ford truck that had once been red but the windborne grit had stripped the paint to reveal the ochre primer beneath. It slowed as the driver spotted them and a bearded face stared at Fishboy perched on the rucksack. He was what Kiwis called a feral or a bogan. His unruly grey hair battled to escape his teacosy cap and there was a gun rack behind the seats. Haast tried the door handle and the door hung on its ancient hinges a few inches short of true.

'Where are you headed?'

He said *head* like *hid* but Haast had been in the Antipodes long enough to make allowances.

'Anywhere.'

'OK. What's with the car?'

'Seized, I have to leave it here.'

The bogan reached between the seats and handed Haast a pair of pliers.

'For the number plates …my name is Sam.'

Haast hesitated to leave Fishboy perched in the seat of the truck but he felt like Sam could be trusted. He snapped the rivets on the number plates quickly and brought them back to the truck.

'Why do you think I need these?' Haast asked.

'I heard about some Irish guy who went berserk in Invercargill. You're a popular man at the moment. I don't care one way or the other, cops never did me any favours.'

Sam put the truck in gear with a grind and they set off into the gloom. Fishboy watched him switch on his cassette player to play 'D.I.V.O.R.C.E.'; he nodded in time to the song. The mournful tune became a soundtrack to darkening glacial fingerprints.

'He likes that stuff – kid's got soul.' His gruff voice came from the depths of his beard. Haast reckoned in a different era that beard would be tied in black ribbons as its owner held a cutlass between his teeth.

'I can drop you in Okarito but I doubt you'll get far. I have a place, you're welcome to stay.'

'I'd like that.'

The beams of the headlights bored into the forming dark. Haast noticed that Sam's middle finger was a stump to the knuckle. Sam caught him in mid-stare.

'Chainsaw, if you were wondering.'

'Are you a forestry worker?'

'I grow things in forests, where they can't be seen from the air.'

'Dope farming.'

'Yup. The stuff wants to grow, so I just give it a nudge.'

The tape turned over.

'Is he yours?' Sam said.

'Yeah, we just met today.'

'In Invercargill.'

'In Invercargill. They have a place there, not a good place.'

'I heard rumours not even the cleaners are local in that place.'

Now Haast had this silent bundle of potential wisdom on his back with his clothes and his laptop and the rest of his responsibilities.

'All I know is that I have a job starting on the North Island in a week. I have to get the kid into some sort of care when I arrive.'

There was no bond there but he would like to see him survive, his link to eternity.

'We should be there in an hour, my missus can feed the boy; I never saw such a quiet baby.' Fishboy curled his lip as if he knew that he was the subject of the conversation. 'Irish, eh?'

'Yeah, came over here a couple of years ago on a tourist visa – still on it.'

'You're not legal then? I know a lot of guys – Islanders, guys with records, you know …'

They pulled into a long sheltered lane and at the top of a hill stood the stone house; a reminder of a dour Scottish settler, long dead. An outside light came on as Sam parked the truck on the gravel by a pile of neatly-stacked firewood.

'OK, you let me do the talking.'

Sam grunted as he dismounted from the truck and he picked up the backpack from inside. Haast got out and hoisted Fishboy from the seat. Sam stopped at the door to unlace his boots so his passenger kicked off his own there too. They entered a room that held chainsaws and overalls hanging on hooks. As Sam opened the door to the next room a waft of warmth hit them and the sound of low music hung in the air. The woman turned from the range to face the new arrivals.

'You collecting again, Sam?'

Even as she said it her eyes fixed on Fishboy. Her face softened and she reached towards the boy. He didn't actively reach out to her but neither did he shrink in Haast's arms.

'Sam, I presume you brought me the most sought after baby on the South Island. I'd expect no less from you.'

'Never could resist a challenge, hon.'

The woman turned on a transistor radio over the sink. An electronic screech was all that came out on any channel.

'That's funny, it worked a few minutes ago when they were looking for information on this little fella.'

'What did they say?'

'That a stranger kidnapped him today from a medical facility. They used words like predator and paedophile. You don't look like a predator to me, young man.'

'His mother put him in that place, for money. I'm just …'

'…a little lost? A lot of people who pass through here are the same. We collect strays. That baby needs feeding. Have you eaten?'

Haast shook his head and found himself ushered to the table. Food would be good. The thick stone walls would deflect any sound or chill and he could rest.

A high clear moon rose over the stone house and silence descended outside.

Mother America

by Nuala Ní Chonchúir

'I come from Fertile, Missouri,' she said, but I didn't believe her. Her car had a bumper sticker that read 'Powered by Jesus'; I didn't believe that either. She had picked me up a few miles outside of Cork city; I'd been hitching for hours with no luck.

'Are you mad, giving a lift to a strange man?' I said, after settling myself into the seat.

'Our Heavenly Father has already made my day,' she said, 'he sent me to make yours. Buckle up.'

'You're from the God Squad; just my fucking luck.' I looked out at the fields, all yellow and lit-up like childhood, then at her. 'What if I'm a murderer? I could jump you right now.'

'Forbidden fruit makes plenty of jam,' she said, smiling her corny, I'm-in-love-with-the-Lord smile. I looked at her longer, even though I didn't want to be looking at her. She had that mad hair that some older American women have: a bushy triangle with a fringe like the top of a broom. She grinned a lot.

'Isn't it boring being a goody-goody? Don't you ever want to go mental and do something really bad?'

'Such as?' She said.

'I dunno. Maybe something like kicking some annoying bastard like me in the head?'

'Now why in Heaven's name would I want to kick you? I'm a pacifist, for one thing, and I don't *hate* you. I don't hate anybody.'

'You're trying to tell me you don't hate child molesters? Come off it!'

'I pray for them. And their victims.' She smiled straight at me and I could tell there was some more nutsy Jesus-wisdom on its way. 'We all need to pray on the days that end with a Y.'

She put her hand on my knee and squeezed it; my Ma used to do that when we drove together in her car. My bloody eyes got all teary. So she wouldn't notice, I leaned forward and examined the Magic Tree that swung from the rear-view. I read the writing on it.

'"This car is prayer conditioned",' I said aloud and flicked the Magic Tree; its piny smell wafted around. 'What a load of puke. They could have at least written something interesting on it. Like, "Take succour, sucker". Or something.'

She laughed. 'That's real funny. You're a smart young man.'

'Do you know what I hate?' I said, my eyes following the broken white lines down the middle of the road until I felt dizzy.

'Hate's a strong word, son; a strong emotion.'

'What I really *dislike* is dogged positivity; it drains the life out of me.' I rolled down the window, needing air. 'And I'm not your son.'

'So, tell me about your Mom.'

'No,' I said, 'I won't.' She swung the car onto the hard-shoulder and sped along it for fifty metres before braking so fast that my whole body jerked forward; I nearly shat myself. 'What the fuck was that?' I shouted.

She gripped my wrist. 'You listen to me. I said tell me about your Mom, so start talking. Start with when she died.'

'How the …? What is this? Is this some kind of piss take?' I looked around me, for what I don't know. 'Who the hell are you?' I asked, pulling at the door handle but it wouldn't open.

'Let's just say I'm your Guardian Angel, sonny.' She let go of my wrist. 'Now talk.'

We sat in silence but I could see she wasn't going to budge. I sighed, I thought about trying to jump out; I looked at cars and trucks and tractors whizzing by. I rolled my fingers on the dash, glanced at her, then closed my eyes and pictured my Ma.

'I could barely stand to visit her,' I said. I glanced sideways at her and she nodded. 'She had that moony face, you know, the way they all look in the end. That was my Ma and she was baldy, like a man. And she was bulge-eyed and so bloody tired looking. Even her eyelashes fell out; it made me feel sick to see her. The pains she had made sort of dents all over her face.' I pointed to my forehead and cheeks, then let my hands fall. 'So I left. I went off and didn't tell her I was going. I rang her after a few days and she was confused, you know? Sort of bewildered. I tried to say "I love you" down the phone; it was all I wanted to say, to explain, but the words choked me, they got stuck. It took three more phone-calls before I got it out and, even then, I whispered it. "I love you, Ma", I said, but I don't even know if she heard.'

'She heard you, Chris. She forgives you and she loves you.'

'You know my name,' I said, stupidly; then I started to cry. I never cry; I hadn't managed a single tear over my Ma until that minute.

The woman leaned across me, her hair swept across my face and it smelt like hay. I half-smiled and went to take her hand, but she opened my door.

'Out now.'

'What?' I said, wiping at the slide of snot and tears around my mouth.

'Out,' she said, gentler this time.

I took my bag from between my legs, threw it out of her car and went to follow it. 'You know my name, at least tell me yours.'

'They call me Mother America,' she said, then she snapped the door shut, and I watched her drive away.

Breeding

by Conor Montague

It's one of those Saturdays sent to test schoolboys in the run-up to exams. Tommy Flaherty ambles up Cappagh Road swinging a length of ash, clipping heads off juvenile dandelions as he goes, sending seed fairies floating over small granite-strewn fields. Slumped shoulders mask recent growth spurts and his acne-speckled face is discoloured on the left side, puffed and swollen around the eye. Two setters throw themselves at Gannon's gate as Tommy passes. He kicks a stone in their direction. It pings off the metal, inspiring a chorus of howls. Mrs Gannon comes out with a basin of dishwater to throw onto the street. She swings it towards the dogs and it splashes across their backs, sending them yelping around the side of the white two-storey farmhouse. She laughs as she turns to go back inside, waving at the youth on the narrow road.

> 'Howya Tommy?'

> 'Howya Mrs Gannon?'

> 'Lovely day.'

> ''Tis.'

Hawthorns bloom white on either side, hunched over stone walls like farmers shooting the breeze, an occasional blush tinting the flowers. A splatter of teal-green dung stains the route Conneely's cattle took earlier. Flies rise as Tommy passes; the sweet perfume an aura as he lashes green tips off the briars peeping out from dense ferns on the verge. Up ahead, a lone magpie pecks at a flattened frog, peeling it off the gravel and flying off as Tommy puts the stick to his shoulder and takes aim, a French delicacy dangling from a scavenger beak.

Sheba barks a welcome from a side-shed as he walks through Moran's gate. Mick comes out of the doorway; he is lean and stocky with a rolling gait. Teenage bristles speckle his chin and upper lip. Dark curly hair drops to where silver studs sparkle on the shoulders of a sleeveless denim jacket. Phil Lynott's iconic image straddles his chest, a precious relic of the Renegade tour.

'Ah the bould Tom Flah, you're just in time.'

'Howya, Mick. Time for what?'

'Have to get rid of the pups; the auld fella's goin' mad.'

High-pitched yaps sound from the shed, accompanied by the deeper barks of the thoroughbred Golden Labrador purchased by Mick with a view to breeding and 'making a few handy quid'.

'Who'll take them?'

Mick looks sideways at Tommy. He registers the bruising on his face before bending to pick up a hurl. He throws a stone into the air and hits it with a dry crack, sending it thirty yards into the thistle-plagued field across the road.

'Take them? Who in the name of Jesus wants those mongrels? And the village full of them. Down to Lallys I should throw the lot of the little fuckers.'

'Snipe again?'

'Who else, that dog is fuckin' deadly ...I mean a Jack Russell, how is it even possible?'

'There's no stoppin' him, sure he has pups with every bitch in the village, unbelievable. You have to admire him, in fairness.'

Mick belts another stone into the air, drops the hurl and walks back to the porch, reaching in to grab a cloth potato sack from the window ledge. Tommy follows him into the shed. Sheba watches Mick place her six offspring into the darkness one by one, all whimpering at the mystery. There is no mistaking the genetic history of the litter. Every pup has the black hair and brown eyebrows of their father.

'Take a fair salesman to sell them as Golden Labradors alright.'

'Don't talk to me, and she locked in the fuckin' shed, I swear to God I thought I was seein' things when I opened the door to Snipe lookin' up at me, and he proud as a fuckin' turkey cock.'

'A wonder ya didn't give it to him?'

'Jesus I tell ya, t'was the shock that saved him; still can't figure it out.'

The two look around the shed for an opening that they know isn't there, like so many have done since this shape-shifting ghost dog joined the village. Mick grabs a length of baling twine off the boiler before patting a bewildered Sheba on the head, closing the door and turning to Tommy.

'What happened the eye?'

'Ah nothin'. Walked into the door of the press, you know the high one in our kitchen, over the sink, corner caught me right under the eye.'

Mick roots through a small pile of rubble by the wall. He picks up half a concrete block, bangs it off the ground a few times and hands it to his friend. He stoops down and selects a slightly larger piece for himself.

'Looks a sore dose.'

''Tis grand, had worse than this.'

Mick leads the way through the lush tunnel of Willhamín's *bóthairín*. The brambles and ferns on either side are sprinkled with grasshopper spit, like a giant sneezed in the night. They walk to the crest of a small hill, then cut across the heather through a gap in the stone wall, following a rabbit-run between the clumps. The beige sack yelps and gyrates in Mick's right hand. He carries half a concrete block under his left arm. Tommy follows behind, watching his friend's black

Doc Martens squelch along the soft ground. He has a stick in his left hand and half a block under his right arm. They pause at a promising boghole. Tommy tests the depth with the ash.

'Hardly enough.'

'Nah.'

'A child can drown in four inches of water you know.'

Mick looks at his friend.

'Well, next time we're drowning children we'll use this one so.'

Their laughter unfurls along the springy heather, lightening the load in Mick's right hand. He speaks back over his shoulder as progress resumes.

'I tell ya one thing, Sheila Joyce might avail of the service. Up the fuckin' stick again, can ya believe it?'

Tommy shakes his head in a gesture of disapproval a Catholic bishop would be proud of. Mick pauses and looks back the way they came. There's a black smudge on his brow, turf dust from the floor of the shed.

'I tell ya, Flah, I wouldn't mind availing of her services.' He looks skywards and loses himself in the vision. A thought brings him back. 'Who's the stallion this time? Hardly Three-Piece again is it?'

'Sure Three-Piece is in London for the past year, doing well too they reckon. Putting down cable he is.'

'Still pullin' his wire all day so. Such a Chrissie-Mongo, I tell ya. When that fucker can get a ride, there's hope for the rest of us.'

Tommy pulls up short, tapping Mick on the left shoulder with the ash.

'I think I know who the father is.'

'Who?'

'Sure isn't it obvious.' He stands facing Mick, block under left arm, stick pointing skywards. 'I can't believe we didn't cop it before.' Mick puts down the sack, takes the block out from under his arm, drops it to the ground, spreads the turf dust across his forehead with the back of his hand and waits, hands on hips, for the revelation. Tommy spreads his arms wide. 'It's Snipe, sure who else? The little fucker's done it again.'

A blast of hilarity shoots shockwaves back down along the *bóthairín* and onto the road. Blackbirds abandon cover in fright, and cattle three fields away pause their grazing to look around. Even Tom Feeney's jackass, known for his ill temper, hee-haws approval from where he is spancilled on the far side of the road. Mick imitates Snipe going at it doggy style, little paws clutching onto Sheila as he hammers away.

'Oh, Snipe, you're so big, give it to me, please, more, more.'

He performs two yelps and a prolonged howl to signify climax. The two are on their knees clutching their midriffs, struggling for breath. Two pups waddle yapping from the sack. Mick makes a clumsy grab for the nearest one.

'Quick, Sheila's sprogs are getting away.'

They roll over onto their backs. Mick holds the escapee to his chest, who piddles down onto Phil Lynott, causing him to fling the pup onto the heather. It's too much for Tommy, lying on his back choking, blue-green world swirling through salty tears, snot and phlegm choking him as he struggles to control his bladder. It is some time before they quieten down, each attempt at speech reignites the furnace until eventually it burns itself out.

Mick reloads the sack, grabs it by the neck and swings it over his shoulder, bending at the knees to pick up the block and tuck it under his arm. They weave their way through gorse and heather towards Boleybeg, pausing now and then to consider potential bog-holes.

'You weren't in yesterday.'

'Nah.'

'How come?'

'Couldn't be arsed.'

'Ya missed fuck all, revision this and revision that, and me sitting there thinking I didn't see any of this shit first time round, all a load of bollocks if you ask me. Sure there's no work anyway, what the fuck would ya want to be studying for?'

'Suppose. English on Wednesday, not much time now. Shouldn't be too bad.'

Mick stops and turns to Tommy, eyebrows arched towards black smudge.

'Not too bad? I tell ya one thing, Flah, I'll ram that exam so far up my arse, I'll be chewing on it for a week, I mean for fuck's sake, sonnets? What in the fuck good are sonnets to anyone, ha? "I wandered lonely as a cloud" ...my fucking arse.'

He turns and leads the way across the bog, shaking his head. A cock robin joins the pilgrimage, hopping frantically from stalk to stalk at a safe distance. Tommy watches the bird as it goes.

'That's Wordsworth.'

Mick stops, stiffening slightly. He leaves the bag down to readjust the block, looking over his left shoulder at his companion.

'What?'

'"I wandered lonely as a cloud", that's Wordsworth.'

Tommy watches Mick turn around, enjoying the indignant expression, the stained forehead, the dramatic pause as he drops his block and picks up the gauntlet.

'Is that a fact now, Wordsworth no less, and did he not write sonnets?'

'I don't know, Shakespeare wrote them anyway, cause that's what we're supposed to read.'

'Are we now, and have you been busy reading the bould Shakespeare in your spare time?'

Tommy laughs, drops his block, and bends forward to pluck a green reed from a clump at his feet. He pulls the end off with a twist of his wrist and places it into his mouth. He looks over the tip at Mick before answering.

'I have in my arse, I just know *The Daffodils* that's all.'

'*The Daffodils*?'

'Yeah, the Wordsworth poem, that's the only one I know.'

Mick spreads his legs and leans back slightly. He glances at the squirming bag at his left foot before turning his attention to Tommy. A bee circles his head like an enemy bomber. He backhands it on the third lap, sending it careening over the heather. The words are more accusation than question.

'What? Ya just love daffodils, is it?'

Tommy looks down at the bag at Mick's feet, takes the reed from his mouth with his right hand, turns and spits to his left. He wipes his lips with the back of his hand before placing the reed in his mouth once more, then looks to where Galway

Bay sparkles in the distance, immersing himself in the view before turning back to Mick.

'The mother loved daffodils, she used to go on about that poem. Sure I'd have to know it, wouldn't I?'

He doesn't wait for an answer but leads the way over the bog, picking his way carefully through a hoof-churned patch as Mick follows, using the same tufts as his friend. When back on solid ground, they pause to survey their surroundings. Black Jack walks a distant field to the south, his bright red *geansaí* Nollag a beacon in the greenery. Mick shakes his head at the sight.

'Jesus he loves that jumper.'

'Wouldn't do to walk in front of Lydon's bull wearing that.'

'That's for fuckin' sure ...what time's the mass tomorrow?'

'Twelve.'

Tommy starts across a wide green patch, Mick by his side.

'Jesus, ya don't feel a year goin'.'

A half-hearted nod is Tommy's only answer as he looks towards the sun, like he's calculating exactly how much feeling fits into a year. A heron rises twenty yards ahead, awkward and graceful. It tucks its head back into its shoulders and lets out a single sharp squawk as it traces a gentle grey arc south along blue canvas, landing near the tall trees behind Gannon's house. Tommy watches its progress.

'Down there his nest is.'

'Bet ya there's a good hole up there,' says Mick, pointing to where they had seen the bird rise, walking ahead of Tommy. A brace of snipe rise ten metres away. They skim rushes, zigzag sharply and alight at the far side of a slight mound. Tommy traces their brief trajectory with his stick.

'Have to get them before they turn, the auld fella'd have them shot from the hip, *BANG BANG*.'

'You any smokes?'

'A nipper.'

Tommy digs into his left-hand pocket and produces half a Major, badly disfigured, and a box of matches. He sparks up the cigarette. The smell of sulphur mingles with tobacco smoke in the still air. He inhales deeply, enjoying the head rush of manhood. He exhales a rapid succession of rings through pursed lips before repeating the process twice, handing the fag to Mick and looking up at a jet streaming towards the North Atlantic. Flotsam trails in its wake, slowly dissipating into nothingness.

'Another bunch gone, lucky fuckers.'

Mick suckles the filter, blowing smoke into the midges swarming around.

'Would ya go?'

'That's for sure, be gone tomorrow if I could, out of this shithole.'

Mick sucks the dregs and flicks the butt into the mud. He watches it smother before turning to his companion.

'Nice head on ya for New York alright, your neck'd be fucked from lookin' up at the buildin's.'

Tommy lurches towards his friend to grab him in a headlock but slips on the soggy ground. Mick swivels to the left and sends him over his right hip onto the heather. Mick kneels with one knee on Tommy's chest and attempts to slap him across the face, careful not to hit the swollen eye.

'You'd want to be faster than that over there, boy, no second chances in New York City.'

Tommy grabs denim shoulders and swings his friend to the right and onto the bag of puppies.

'Jesus mind, ya'll kill the pups.'

Mick gets his feet under him and springs from the ground like a kid goat, twisting in mid-air and landing with a foot each side of the squealing bundle. Tommy climbs to his feet, catching his breath. Mick twists the top of the sack to prevent escape. They walk to where they had seen the heron rise. Sure enough, there is a decent sized pond, about four foot in diameter and a couple of foot deep in the middle, half-way up Tommy's staff. Green rushes encircle the brown water, and a smattering of bog-cotton sprinkles its way northwards towards McComisky's. Mick twirls the package anticlockwise, leaves it down, opens the sack and drops his block into the litter. The frightened whimpers make Tommy flinch.

'Jesus will ya mind, you'll hurt the poor fuckers.'

'Do ya really think it matters at this stage?'

'No point making it worse.'

Tommy opens the sack and places his block gently in among the litter, catching sight of squashed little faces. Eyes squint towards the bright light, yelps intensifying. He closes the sack and turns to his friend, who is pulling a length of yellow baling twine from his back pocket.

'Is there no one who'll take them?'

'What's on ya, if ya can't stomach it just wait down there.'

Mick gestures towards the road. Adulthood rests easy on his young shoulders, its weight expanding his barrel chest. Tommy heaves the bundle to Mick's feet.

'Course I can stomach it, just a pity that's all.'

Tommy steps closer to the boghole. A water-boatman skims across his shadow. Two dragonflies chase one another in circles, swooping and touching the surface sporadically, emerald and scarlet beneath blurred wings. Mick's shadow merges from behind and the sack is hoisted into the middle of the pool. It lands with a dull gulp. Skimming insects surf splash-waves towards the edges, where they are absorbed by the soft peat. Tadpoles seek the slimy green cloak by the far side of the pond, tails piercing the glistening skin of the surface.

The bag floats momentarily; trapped air fighting dead weight as soft water gently seeps through the cloth. Panicked squeals sound as the litter sinks slowly, fighting inevitable silence as best they can; threads of tiny bubbles in their wake. The sack finds rest on the mud bed. Visibility is regained as the disturbed sediment slowly settles. The last of the air loosens the baling twine as it leaves the bag. They watch as one tiny black snout pokes through the slight opening, wriggling desperately into wet embrace. Mick shakes his head, exhaling loudly.

'For fuck's sake, will ya look at this fucker.'

'Ya didn't tie it properly.'

Mick turns to Tommy with a snarl. 'Course I fuckin' tied it properly.'

He calms instantly at the sight of Tommy's smirk.

'There's always gonna be a bit of give. It'll be grand.'

He turns to face the pond as the pup's head breaks the surface, hysterical black eyes under brown eyebrows. He calls Mick's bluff with a whimper, and swims dazed in a circle like a dwarf sea-lion. Mick reaches over and grabs the stick from Tommy's hand.

'For fuck's sake.'

He places the point of the staff on the pup's crown and pushes him under. As they wait for the bubbles to cease a sibling surfaces dead with lips curled back over virgin white teeth, looking like it grasped the comedy in its dying breath. Mick loses concentration and his charge pops up once more and flounders towards the edge.

'Ya little fucker.'

Mick takes no chances this time. He spears the pup in the side with the ash and drives him down into the murk, leaving his weight on the stick until he feels it pierce baby ribs. He looks wide-eyed at Tommy before pulling the shaft sharply from the water with a loud 'Yeah!' Tiny red bubbles shoot to the surface, tingeing the brown water. A curlew sounds a keen from across the bog. It rises in wistful intensity, peaks and restarts.

The two shift position in silence, moving around the pond until their shadows disappear and close the window to the death below. A tinted sky is mirrored on the water's skin. A solitary corpse floats among wine-coloured clouds. They watch as the traffic returns. Nymphs, water beetles and tadpoles invade the murky crypt as water boatmen and pond skaters skim across the heavens. As they turn for home, Tommy spots a camouflaged frog watching from the edges, pulsing white throat compromising its position. He says nothing.

They walk in silence back over the bog and down

through the *bóthairín*. The tommy-gun staccato of a roused tractor pulses from the direction of Barna. Mick glances sideways at Tommy before he speaks.

'Hear your auld fella's back on the beer.'

'He is.'

'Since when?'

'Thursday night.'

Tommy looks away from Mick, down across the fields to where crows riot around the small copse of spruce beside Tom Paraicín's cottage. He swings his staff upward with his left hand, cleaving the prickly bulbous head off a thistle, sending it soaring over a stumpy blackthorn into an adjacent field. Mick's eyes follow the missile then return to his friend.

'You're very quiet.'

'Just thinkin' that's all.'

'They're better off, Tom. Sure nobody wanted the fuckers. If nobody wanted you ..."

Tommy passes no remark, decapitating another thistle. They continue in silence until the bóthairín widens into the road. Tommy swirls to face his friend, causing him to pull up abruptly.

'Do ya know what the tragedy is, Mick?' He looks into Tommy's face but can't hold his stare and shifts from foot to foot. Tommy grabs his shoulders, forcing him to meet his gaze. 'Do you know what the real fuckin' tragedy is?' Mick shakes his head. 'How many males were in that litter?'

'Four.'

Tommy loosens his grip on Mick's shoulders and stands back, a grimace tightening his lips.

'Those four dogs will never get to enjoy the one god-given gift they possess.'

'How'd ya mean?'

A robin flutters to the top of a hawthorn and proclaims their guilt to the village. Brendan Lally speeds past in his white Renault 4, leaving the road briefly at the hump of Martín's Hill. He beeps a greeting upon landing before disappearing around the bend in a gust of gravel. Tommy turns back to Mick with a forlorn look on his bruised face.

'Don't ya get it Mick? Those poor fuckers will never get to lick their own balls. The one thing that makes them better than us and we took it away from them. Fuck your Macbeth and all that shite. That's a real tragedy.'

Tommy guffaws, infecting his companion instantly. Mick, bent double by the sucker-punch, places a hand on Tommy's shoulder as he fights for breath, taking advantage of the veil to pull him into a brief tight hug, before pushing him away and punching hard into his right bicep.

The Disposable Girl

by Máire T. Robinson

Disposable cameras contain a battery, but customers forget. Sometimes I watch from the window as they flick through their photos outside. They smile to themselves or shake their heads. Some vow to lose a few pounds, others not to make that peculiar face in future. At home, they place the pictures in an album or a frame. The AA battery is barely used. It was only needed to spark brief flashes of light. But they never ask for it back.

There's been an increase in the number of disposable cameras we get in for processing. It seems strange, given so many people have digital cameras these days, but they spend so much money on the things they don't trust themselves to use them. They go to their friend's wedding or grandchild's christening and capture the moment with a disposable camera. Owners unworthy of their possessions. Like a sofa in the good room with the plastic covering still on it.

I bought an SLR camera when I started my photography course. I used black and white film so I could use the college darkroom for processing. Some people find it laborious. Why bother learning about aperture settings and focus and light readings when you can let a point and shoot camera do the work for you? I wanted to take his photograph, but he wouldn't let me.

He looked straight through me with those dark eyes, 'Do you want to steal my soul?'

I suppose in a way, I did.

The disposable cameras sit on the counter, waiting for me to uncover their secrets. I take the first one from the pile, crack open the plastic seals and pull it apart. I remove the film and set it aside for processing. I peel back the sticker to find the battery inside, nestled like a hidden pearl. I throw it into the large bucket under the counter, full of other semi-used batteries. I leave the dismantled parts of the camera to one side for recycling, grab another camera from the pile and repeat the process.

When I started working here, I admit I took a certain voyeuristic pleasure in seeing other people's photographs, but after a while they all started to look the same. Each day the processing machine spits out an endless stream of christenings, birthdays, holidays and weddings. It's uncanny how the same smiles and poses are repeated. Subjects adhere to the same template, chanting 'cheese' in unison. They contort their mouths into the required shape, as though their teeth were not for tearing flesh apart, but merely for smiling.

We rarely see anything out of the ordinary these days. Mike, my boss, says we used to get a lot more nude shots. I suppose the advent of digital technology has been a blessing for the amateur pornographer. Now they can sidestep the developing process and spare their blushes. The odd one still crops up now and again. Last month I developed a set of a naked girl. Her face was expressionless, her eyes dead. She couldn't have been more than seventeen. I wondered what her name was and who she was trying to please on the other side of the camera. The photographs were never collected. I added them to the Unclaimed drawer.

It happens more than you might imagine, people failing to collect their photographs. We date the envelope and keep them for three months. If nobody collects them in that time, we throw them out. Sometimes if I see one I like, I sneak it home and paste it into an album. I like to turn its pages and look at my family of abandoned rejects. A Japanese girl at the Cliffs of Moher, a cock-eyed boy in front of the elephant enclosure at Dublin Zoo, an aged couple perched on a picnic blanket, both naked apart from their smiles and sunhats.

I check the photos emerging from the processing machine for smudges or other defects before putting them in envelopes. The usual smiling faces and landscapes are spat out in succession. Fine, fine, fine …until a beautifully composed set appears. They are of a girl wearing a green dress. Her skin is translucent, pale, flawless. Her black hair hangs down to her waist. She stands in front of a lake. Behind her, two tall trees lean towards each another, meeting at the top in an embrace of entwined branches. The photographs are taken from the other side of the lake so that the image of the girl and the trees is captured twice; in the image itself and in a mirror image that appears in the still water. I decide I will take a closer look when the last one …but the last one in the set isn't of the girl. It seems to be of the person who took the photographs, reluctantly agreeing to appear in the final frame. He stares out, eyes burning through the photograph; a vengeful spirit, finally captured.

It was difficult to hold eye contact with him then. I felt as though I could turn into a pillar of salt. His black eyelashes were longer, thicker and darker than mine. They framed his eyes. Two inky pools. An invitation to drown.

He said he was studying sculpture.

'What made you want to study photography?' He asked.

'I like taking photos.'

He laughed as though I had said it to be funny. 'You don't say?'

On my lunch break, I walk up Shop Street to a sandwich bar. The street is heaving with shoppers, tourists and buskers. I walk past a man taking his wife's photograph. They are decked out in typical tourist attire, matching raincoats and a huge golf umbrella. It is a sunny day and most of the other people on the street are wearing T-shirts, but I suppose you can never be too careful. He has positioned her in front of a bakery. It is a fairly non-descript building, so I wonder why he chose it as the background for his shot. Perhaps he really likes bread. Who knows?

'Smile, honey!' He orders.

His wife obliges and I realise I am in the frame. As I duck to avoid being in the shot, I wonder how many times I have been an accidental subject. In countries all over the world, are there pictures where I am a blurred figure who failed to avoid the shutter's click?

After lunch, I pick up where I left off operating the processing machine and putting the photographs into envelopes, ready for collection. The tinny sound of the bell announces a customer's arrival. I peek out, thinking it might be him, but it is a middle-aged man in a suit. He is greeted by Mike. Chitchat and talk of rain. The man has come to collect his digital prints. There is a noticeable absence of anticipation in these customers. No sense of excitement or dread about receiving their photos back. They have already examined the pictures on their camera screens the moment after taking them. They have already edited the imperfections: red eyes, double chins, odd expressions and other deletable crimes.

I flick through the photos of the girl again, stopping on the last one to study his face. Five years haven't changed him much. Back then I never thought I'd end up in a place like this, developing holiday snaps for minimum wage. But this is all temporary. I'll open my own studio one day. It's not like I've stopped taking photographs. Mike lets me come in before work to use the lab for processing. It's not the same as working in a darkroom, but at least it's something. I miss the college darkroom and the hours spent in twilight processes, studying negatives and manipulating light and shade. I miss guiding prints through their succession of baths and seeing the images emerge through ripples of water. I even miss the vinegar smell of the developing chemicals on my fingers. It would linger there for days, like a stubborn memory refusing to fade. Everything is brightly lit here. The machines take care of the processing. It is a lab, not a studio. A place of science, not of art.

When we met up for a drink, he told me it was his birthday.

'I would have got you a present if I'd known.'

He shook his head and laughed at the idea. 'It's only a birthday.'

He was 24. Six years older than me, but it may as well have been a century. He talked about photographers, film-makers, artists and musicians I'd never heard of. He had travelled everywhere. He had seen everything. Sometimes he leaned back as he spoke, so that his eyes were in shadow and I could just make out his lips and his hands. When he spoke, his hands were never still. He sliced the air for emphasis or clasped them together. He gestured with his palms facing upwards, like Jesus imploring his disciples. I drank him in silently, wishing I had my camera to capture him.

He was staying with a friend, until he found his own place, he said. He led me into the sitting room. When he undressed, his body was taut and porcelain smooth, like a marble statue. The room was lit by an electric fire. It shined garishly but gave no heat. I wished the room was pitch black.

That we could find each other through touch alone. That I didn't have to see him seeing me. We lay on the floor, the fake fire casting strange green shadows on our flesh.

I try to imagine myself in his photographs. I picture myself in the dark-haired girl's place, standing in front of a lake and smiling at him through a lens. But I can't maintain this image for long. I become a shadow on the edges. Indistinct as smog. Or the idea of something but not the thing itself. Captured by accident.

The next morning, he folded up the quilt and rested it on a chair. He frowned at the floral print carpet. One of the blue roses had a blood red petal. He stamped on it with his foot like a bull, grinding all trace of it into the ground.

'Well, I suppose we'll see each other around,' he said at the front door, giving me a clumsy kiss that missed my lips and grazed my cheek. He must have left college, moved somewhere else. I only saw him once after that, about a week later in town. I looked at him expectantly, but he walked past me like I was a ghost.

It is not him but the girl who comes to collect the photos. She arrives alone, while Mike is on his break and I am behind the counter. She hands me her ticket and smiles. I pat the pocket of my jeans. The extra copy of his photo is inside. I take her money and hand her the envelope. I want to say something, but can't think what. As she turns to leave, I feel a twinge of shame, as though I have stolen from her.

'Would you like some batteries?'

She turns, surprised, 'Batteries?'

I nod, 'We've so many. Just going to waste.'

Ice-Cream Man

by Paul McMahon

'Lavery's pub,' I said to the taxi driver, as I slammed the door shut.

'Where are you from?' he said, giving me a quick but penetrating glance, as the taxi pulled away from my father's house just off the Andersonstown Road in West Belfast. It was a sunny Sunday afternoon. I was going for the cure.

'I'm from here,' I said, exaggerating my accent. 'I've been gone a rake of years, but I grew up here.'

'That's some day, n'it?' He was about forty, short hair brushed into a side-shade and a moustache. He nodded his head in rhythm with the words.

We drove up the street. Two boys about ten years old were playing football. As we went past, one of them threw the ball over the taxi. It rebounded off the kerb and hit the car.

'The wee fuckin' toe rag,' the driver hissed, beeping his horn.

'Aye, yer ma,' shouted one of the boys, giving him the middle finger.

'Wee fuckin' muckers,' said the driver, as we turned the bend. 'Give'em another ten years and they'll be fuckin' lunatics. A mate of mine,' he went on, 'used to live in this estate. He told me a story once ...well, before I tell you that story, I'll tell you about my mate just to let you know what kind of a fella he is. He was with his mates, in the front garden drinking Buckfast. His ma and da were away, hot sunny day, had the music blasting out into the front garden. Ye know what'a mean like?' I nodded. 'A funeral cortege came down the street. Yer man jumps up and runs inside and changes the record to 'Going Underground' by the Jam. Aye, so that's the fella was telling me the story. There was a fella lived in this estate here and he knew that his wife was fucking a seventeen year old kid.'

The cab was heading over Finaghy Bridge going towards Finaghy Road south. On a wall was painted, 'Ulster says No but the man from Delmonte says Yes'.

'And the other thing he knew,' the driver went on, 'was that, every day, at five thirty, his wife came home from work, through the front door, walked up the stairs, went into the bathroom, sat down on the toilet and took a piss. She always kept the door open. At twenty-five minutes past five, before she came in from work, the husband went up into the attic. The attic door was one of those square flaps in the ceiling right in front of the bathroom door. Do you know the ones I mean?'

'Aye,' I said, 'I know the ones.'

'Well, he went up there and tied a rope around the rafters and a rope around his neck and waited. At five thirty his wife came in, walked down the hall, up the stairs, under him standing over the square hole in the ceiling, went into the bathroom, sat down and started taking a piss. His intention, of course, was to jump down and hang himself in front of her so that she would be mentally scarred for life. He dropped down through the hole but he tied the rope too long. He landed on the floor and broke his leg. She finished taking her piss, flushed the toilet, and as she stepped over him, she looked down at him and said, "You can't even hang yourself right", then walked out the door.'

'Fuck sake,' I said.

'Aye, and the biggest bummer for him was that he was the ice-cream man. Word spread y'see. Two months later, with his leg in a plaster Paris, he was out driving his ice-cream van around the estate again.'

'Is that legal?'

'This is West Belfast, what the fuck has legal got to do with it? Nothing here is legal. I'm not legal. He had to go back to work, it's as simple as that. So there he was, in the plaster Paris, going about in the ice-cream van and fellas like my mate, the 'Going Underground' fella, were going up to him and asking for ninety-nines with extra flakes, extra hundreds and thousands and *extra rope.*'

I laughed.

'Aye,' he shouted, 'you might think it's funny …'

'Ah, no,' I said.

'Do you know that film with Colin Farrell?' The driver said, as we passed the King's Hall. 'The one where he goes into a shop and starts talking about love at first sight to the girl working there behind the counter? Then, just when we think he is going to ask her out, he punches her in the face and robs the till?'

'Aye,' I said, '*Intermission*.'

'I was in a cinema, in Belfast, watching that film, with a Dutch friend of mine, right?' He nodded to me and I nodded back. 'Well, when Farrell punched her in the face the whole fuckin' cinema burst out laughing. My Dutch friend turned to me and said, "In Holland we would not laugh at that. That is not funny."'

'Goes to show ye,' I said.

'Goes t'show ye fuckin' what? It goes t'show ye that we Irish are a bunch of malicious bastards.'

We pulled up outside Lavery's Pub. I was sure he could see the beads of sweat on my forehead. Malicious me had also laughed at that scene in the cinema. I wasn't Dutch and I was guilty as sin, and he knew it. He had 'Mum' tattooed on his knuckles. I gave him the cash and bolted for the bar.

When I told the bartender about 'Going Underground' and extra rope, I was rendered blind by pints and pints of burning tears of delicious, malicious laughter.

Shapeshifter

by Aideen Henry

Sexual tension creates chaos yet you'd be lost without it. What does it mean when you feel it with a stranger? That your marriage is over? That you no longer love or desire your wife? Yet if you weren't unavailable would you feel it at all? What does it mean when you see your wife's senses prick, her eyelids open wider, her pupils dilate, the pulse in her neck start to bound? That the person across from her excites her, yes. But does that mean, like slicing a cake of a finite size, that there is less for you, that she feels less for you? Do you want her to stay with you while she dreams of him, make love with you fuelled by desire for him? And if she does stay, is that through a sense of duty to you or is it love? Is that insecurity or is it love?

Christopher stirs brown sugar crystals into his americano, while his mind skirts the edges of these thoughts. He has the purplish tinge to his cheeks typical of an ex-drinker. He pings the spoon on the side of the cup, lays it on the saucer and waits. The sugar flitting against the porcelain sounds like ceramic wind-chimes wafting in a breeze. He checks his watch. His leather jacket creaks and the bunch of keys hanging from his jeans jangles.

He first met Elizabeth at a student party twenty years before. He remembers posters of Muhammad Ali and Che Guevara above two black bikes locked in the hallway. The sitting room was in semi-darkness, all the furniture removed apart from cushions scattered around the floor. The music boomed and a red bulb from a lamp in the corner cast low light, outlining couples sitting and lying about the room.

In the kitchen, he leaned against the fridge in a lethargic haze, sipping his bottle of beer, his mind lolling after the frenzied violin reels earlier in the pub. He didn't know he was looking until she walked in. Widely spaced lazy brown eyes and tousled long hair. Tall but soft and curvy so you could imagine melting into her. Their eyes met and she smiled but not just at him.

'That'll be five pounds entry to the first class carriage.' He said. She turned towards the sitting room. 'Hey, hang on, you can't go in there.'

'Why not?' Her voice was deep and resonant. 'Is it a £10 entry there?'

'Worse. No fee but you'll come out changed. A different person.'

'Maybe I want to be a different person.'

'Righteo, so, I'll have a beer here waiting for you when your transformation is complete.'

Her lips parted and she floated into the sitting room. His thumb twisted his marriage band absently. He stared at the doorway.

'Have you any Harp?' she said.

He jumped when she spoke from the other doorway; he opened a bottle by slamming it down on the edge of the table with his palm and watched as she took a long draught of it.

'So, what brings you here? Are you a student?'

'Just finished finals today. We're on the beer.'

She clinked bottles with his, looked at his ring and raised the bottle to her mouth for another slug.

'I see you're no student.' She said, looking around the room.

He ran his hands through his hair, caught. 'No.'

'Good. That means you have transport?'

'Well, yes, of a kind.'

'Let's get out of here so.'

He unlocked the helmet from his motorbike and took the spare helmet for her from the rear pannier box. His four months with her began that night. In all of that time there was always something beyond reach with Elizabeth. Some part of her that remained closed to him. As closed to him emotionally as she was open to him physically. He never knew whether it was that he had reached the limit of her. That he expected something from her she didn't have to give. Or maybe there was something withheld. She was everything Martha wasn't.

At that time Martha was besotted with baby Katie. When it came to bathing, feeding, dressing and playing with the baby, she was the expert. He could do nothing right. He felt like a cuckold, an extra in his own home. One afternoon he finished early at the factory and brought home a cake and flowers. He crept into the house. As he walked up the carpeted stairs, placing each foot before transferring his weight onto it, he could hear her voice, half-whispering, half-singing and tender, so tender. The bedroom door was ajar. Martha was lying in bed naked with Katie in a nappy facing her. The baby's hands were holding Martha's cheeks and Martha was stroking the baby's face. Her voice had a softness he had never heard before. The look in her eyes naked, exposed. He slipped back down the stairs and left the house. After that the baby seemed to swell, gluttonously fattening on its monopoly. By the time he met Elizabeth, in Christopher's mind baby Katie had a head like a marshmallow with two buried currants for eyes, and five ripples of flesh along each thigh.

Martha's interest in him centred upon his chances of promotion at the factory, a checklist of what else they could afford to buy for the baby and discussions on when it would be best for her next to conceive. A sister or brother for baby Katie. If she could see herself. Gone was the birdlike, tight-bodied working-class girl he had married. In her place was a shapeshifter in leggings and long T-shirts, originally loose but now at the limit of their elasticity.

For those four months Elizabeth's body was home to him. She liked clear space. In her bedroom there was nothing extra to her needs; no clutter, no frilly things, no fripperies of any kind. It was like sleeping in a model room in a design museum. He kept thinking spectators would walk in and pass comment, pointing at him, the only untidy object in the room. Unlike other women, Elizabeth had little interest in meals out, meeting friends or going to the pictures together. She was suspicious of being given flowers or presents of any kind. She preferred to make love without alcohol, a new experience for him. There was no taboo, judgement or fear. Just trust, curiosity and exploring each other's textures and contours. Bliss. She wanted from him what Martha didn't. She was even reluctant to talk.

Christopher waited, always expecting her to complain or to look for some return or commitment from the pleasure she gave him. It never happened. Free of the mundane habits of living together, they shared only sensuous touch. Words lacked the eloquence of their bodies. That summer they spent their stolen hours in her bedroom, on the sand dunes of deserted beaches or in the forest with a picnic.

Elizabeth's new job transferred her to London. If she was upset to be leaving him she didn't show it.

'Ten years from now,' she asked the ceiling, 'where will you be?'

Her head was thrown back on the pillow, beads of sweat on her forehead. He slid out of her limp and rolled onto his back.

'You know where I'll be.'

'How could I know?'

'I'll be precisely where I am now. Stuck in this town, married with a wife as big as a house and an 11-year-old daughter playing catch-up.'

'You don't know for sure.'

'I can tell you where you'll be too. Married, I'd say, with one or two kids of your own.'

'Oh, will I now? How well you think you know me. Would you like to bet on it?'

They agreed to meet in ten years, on New Year's Eve in the Castle Hotel, Killiney.

Now it has been twenty years. Elizabeth walks past the coffee shop on the far side of the road so she can get a look at him before he sees her. That must be him sitting at the window, a shock of white hair in the place of his black curls. Obviously lost in thought. She had tried Googling him but no images came up apart from the court one, in which half his face was covered. The drizzle lightens; she closes her umbrella and crosses the street. She knows her figure is fuller than twenty years before yet she feels she has the same energy in her stride. Wearing a tailored navy trouser suit with an elaborate turquoise ceramic neck pendant and matching earrings, she stands for a moment with her back to a doorway next door to the coffee shop, looking out on the street view that he faces. A rogue memory returns to her. Sitting on the train having just left him all those years before, her body freshly fucked and wanton. The mind has many veils to cover and uncover, she thinks. It has strange time locks too.

She grips the steel handle of the heavy glass door and wonders about the protocol on greeting. Handshake? Too formal. Kiss on the cheek? Too casual. Kiss on the lips? Too intimate. Hug? Too needy. Feck. Let him decide. Christopher stands up. He looks stunned and sheepish as he moves towards her. Handshake and the other hand on her shoulder blade. Friendly. But not a glimmer of the sexual. He has shrunk. Pity. She just realises what hopes she had harboured.

'Your lovely long hair,' he says, 'you've cut it.'

'Oh, yes,' she says touching her hair, 'it's easier to manage.'

She feels like she has damaged something belonging to him.

They fumble behind two small menus and she orders green tea and he another americano. They look out the window and watch as a woman turns to her little boy and wags her index finger in his face. The boy doesn't react but looks past his mother at Elizabeth until his mother tugs him by the arm to walk on with her. His eyes are locked on Elizabeth to the last. Rain streams down the window.

'So how have you been anyway? You're still married?' Says Elizabeth.

'Yes. That's a good one, isn't it? Now that divorce is in, I wouldn't want it.' Elizabeth's eyes dart from his face to her hands. Christopher shifts in his seat. 'But that's just me. My circumstances. Who am I to say?'

Elizabeth sits upright in her metal chair.

'Martha's doing very well, isn't she?'

'Fair play to her, she is. You wouldn't know her from the woman she was twenty years ago.'

'No. You wouldn't, would you? I was surprised.'

'How?'

'Oh, didn't I say in the email? We met at her exhibition in London. Must have been five years ago. Justin was looking for a piece for the bank foyer and her paintings are wonderful.'

'That was just after the accident. Katie was in hospital.'

'I particularly like her photography. All those rock faces and canyons.'

'I thought she was going to leave me. That's when she told me,' Christopher says.

'She must have done a study of geology. Fascinating.'

'She knew. All that time she knew. She just waited. "I waited for you to come back to me," she said, "and you never did."'

'And then there's the abstracts. Her use of gold foil.'

'She's a bigger person than me. Bigger than I ever could have been.'

'We discussed her ink drawings with her. She really is talented.'

'The only way she would stay is if I went to John of God's and got myself sorted out. I was lucky to have a family to go back to, never mind a job.'

'Of course you never met Justin, did you? A fantastic chap. Loves the arts, theatre, painting, literature.'

The waitress arrives with the tray. She wipes the table with a stained blue J-cloth smelling of bleach, before placing their coffee and tea before them.

'Would yiz like anythin' else to go with that?'

'No, no thank you.' Elizabeth says in a tight voice.

'No problem.' She waddles back to the counter, the sound of her tights rubbing, and picks up the phone to continue chatting to her friend.

After a few moments Christopher sits up straight.

'So did you go to the Castle Hotel, in Killiney?'

She looks at him suspiciously.

'The ten year bet, remember? New Year's Eve?'

'Did you?' She says.

'No. I couldn't.'

Silence again. Christopher tries once more. 'You mentioned your husband, Justin.'

'Ex-husband.'

'Sorry, yes. What happened?'

'Well. Let's see if I can I summarise it in less than three sentences.' She sips her tea and returns the cup to its saucer. 'OK. We met, we fucked, we loved, we married, then we split and now he's with someone else.'

'Oh. I ...I'm sorry.'

'I don't think this was a good idea. I'm being rude now. I'd better go.'

Elizabeth gets up and puts on her coat. Christopher stands also, his keys rattling.

'But I thought ...'

'You thought what?' She replies. 'That we could pick up where we left off before? Not likely.'

'Not like that. I thought we could meet as human beings, as people who shared something together in the past.'

'Look, I'm sorry, this was a mistake. I'm too old to pretend. I can't do this.' Christopher looks forlorn. Elizabeth takes her turquoise scarf from the back of the chair, doubles it over and pushes the two ends through the loop, drawing it up to her neck. She runs her hand around the back of her neck as though to free her hair, forgetting it is short. 'There is no going back, Christopher. People or people's circumstances always change. Be happy with what we had and what you have now that you nearly lost.'

She holds out her hand and shakes his, releasing she is keen to escape before there is time to change the deal. Elizabeth pulls the heavy glass door open and steps out on to the street, now shiny in the sun after the rain.

The strange thing is, she thinks, that it seems she won the bet. Not so much because she is now divorced and childless, but because his life, though he is still married, has changed utterly. Whereas she feels close to being the person she was when they parted. She's not sure why she agreed to meet. What did she expect? What they did best together was horizontal and wordless. All their other interactions just preliminaries, things to be gotten out of the way. Drives, walks and conversations to get beyond. All to get to that glorious physicality, that sensate focus. Now he's a shadow of a man if ever there was one, hanging onto his wife's coat tails.

She enters a shopping centre, steps on the escalator and watches herself in the mirror as it carries her to the first floor. Relationships. So overrated. Together they had the only part of any value with none of the attendant tedium. Mad that the physical is regarded as base, when it's the pinnacle. The rest just wrangling; a contest for power played out over a lifetime together – where life throws obstacles in each person's path to keep it interesting.

In the hairdressers she takes a seat at the sink. With her head basking in hot water she relaxes into the assistant's hands, as her scalp is scratched all over.

'Day off today?'

'Yes, a day off.'

'Doin' anythin' for the weekend?'

'No, no plans for the moment.'

Relieved to stop talking, she savours the rhythmic pressure on her scalp as a second shampoo is applied and afterwards a peach-smelling conditioner that is massaged in by the soft pads of the hairdresser's fingers. She presses her head into the hairdresser's hands like a Labrador pressing a hand for affection. Seated in front of a mirror having her hair cut, she watches the owner of the salon sitting nearby brushing out her own hair out after a colouring, her movements similar to a cat washing its face.

After the cut and blow dry she makes her way back to her car. Walking past a row of houses with tidy hedges of copper beech, she runs her fingers along hedge tops as if reading Braille, looking for sense. When she reaches her car she realises she left her umbrella in the coffee shop. She doesn't go back.

A Monkey is for Life

by Dara Ó Foghlú

Coley McGuire's luck turned for the better when he lost his hand to the sawmill. He said as much to Senan Clarke, sitting at the bar in Clarke's one afternoon, a smile and a feed of whiskey holding him up, and a monkey just as drunk on the next barstool.

'Luck is a fickle mistress,' Senan said. 'You can't depend on her from one day to the next.'

It occurred to Coley that barmen were always coming out with pointless truisms like this. They must spend their entire lives cataloguing them, he thought.

Coley lost his hand to the round-baler in the cattle-feed factory by the river in Boyle. He grew up there, and the town showed little sign of ever letting him go. After finishing school, thanks to his teachers' gentle encouragement and comprehensive beatings, he secured a job at the mill, where his father had worked until the moment he died. It seemed natural to everyone, including Coley, that he should inherit his father's job as well as his crumbling house. Although he didn't like his job feeding silage into the baler, it had never occurred to Coley that a job was meant to be enjoyed, so he worked hard, if a little distractedly. He day-dreamed about exotic places, and what it would be like to live in a country where the rain and wind didn't chase you out of bed, all the way to work, and into the pub every day. In documentaries he had seen about Africa, it was always too sunny even for a T-shirt, everyone drank out of coconuts, and the women wore beads and colourful necklaces, if they wore anything at all.

One day, feeding bales into the sawmill, the machine bit into him and took his hand off. Some months later, telling the story to Dave Murphy, of Murphy's pub, he explained that he was somewhere else altogether. The Congo, possibly. He went on to tell the barman how he had pulled his arm back from the mouth of the automatic guillotine only to find his hand was missing – gobbled up by the same contraption that had taken many a hand before Coley's, and would, most likely, take many more yet. Men around the plant were nervous working on it and had taken to calling it 'Jaws'.

When Coley's hand came under the angled blade it was taken off at the wrist without interrupting the beat of Jaws' rhythm. It was only when the foreman saw Coley holding his arm aloft, baffled by where the rest of it could have gotten to, that he hit the emergency stop. While the flat plain of his wrist was hosing blood, some men ran to get bandages to staunch the wound, others ran to telephone the ambulance, and the foreman went looking in the cogs and ratchets for the missing hand. Amongst all this commotion, Coley stood alone on the workfloor in a puddle of his own blood, still not sure what was going on.

That realisation would come when he was wheeled into hospital, accompanied by the pain and the shock. Laid out on a gurney, looking down at the stains on his white runners, Coley thought about how much blood he had lost and how much might be still left inside him. The tank was probably half-empty by his reckoning, and he began to rattle with panic, so the nurse gave him morphine to settle him down. As he was about to pass out, he noticed his hand, disconnected and grey on a tray of ice beside him; it looked like a prop – more like a mould of wax or rubber than his own flesh and bone.

When he woke up he was back in one piece again, his hand heavily wrapped in gauze. A dark-skinned doctor with unreasonably white teeth and a scarlet turban stood smiling beside the bed.

'Welcome back, Mister McGuire.'

Coley had never seen a man with such dark skin before. And only once in a James Bond film with Roger Moore had he seen a man wearing a turban.

'Where am I?'

'You're in hospital.'

'Right. What country?'

'Ireland, of course.'

'Oh. And me hand?'

'Yes. Please do not try to move it yet. As you can see, I have been able to reattach it. Please, no thanks are necessary.'

The doctor waited for Coley to say something.

'Thank you, doctor.'

'You are most welcome. Unfortunately when we sew the tendons, nerves, and muscles back together not all of them take and there is nothing anyone can do about this. So you will not be enjoying the full movement of your hand as you once had, but, all things considered, you are a very lucky fellow.'

Coley couldn't move his thumb after the operation. It was locked into a thumbs-up position. Try as he might, he could move it no more than the point of a needle in any direction, and the effort of it brought him to tears and exhaustion. He cried there in the hospital bed because he knew everyone would mock him for it. They were like that in Boyle.

After the accident, Coley was given a job in packaging. The money was the same but it was the type of job they gave to women and pansy-men. It was only later, upon seeing the succession of zeros written on his insurance claim cheque, that everything changed for Coley McGuire. His frozen thumb would be a constant reminder of how rich he had become. Let everyone laugh, he thought, he would be laughing harder. He promptly quit the mill, giving his boss and co-workers the thumbs up as he left.

The smartest thing to do with the money, he decided, would be to buy two new cars – neither of which he put tax or insurance on – and a monkey called Panther.

Coley had the local tailor fashion a tweed jacket and matching paddy-cap for Panther to keep out the cold. When they tugged the monkey into his outfit, the tailor remarked how much like Coley's late father he looked.

'He's certainly hairy enough,' the tailor said. 'All he's missing is the cigarette hanging from his lip.'

'Here. Watch this,' Coley said. He rummaged in his pockets for a box of Benson and Hedges. He drew out two cigarettes and put one in his mouth. 'Panther? Watch Coley, okay?'

Then he handed the second cigarette to Panther, who put it between his lips and started puffing his cheeks.

'Amazing,' the tailor said.

Wherever they went people wanted to see Coley's monkey. Shamie Hughes, owner of Hughes' Pub, told Coley one day that business had been booming since they started drinking there.

'People love to see that monkey of yours. He's like a hairy leprechaun or something.'

'I suppose he is.'

'Tell me, Coley, how did you go about spending your claim money?'

'Well,' Coley said, 'I got myself a Datsun, which is a good, sturdy car and I don't expect it will ever give me any trouble. And I got a Delorean too for the craic. It has the neighbours pure thick with jealousy.'

'But why the monkey?' Shamie asked, looking from Coley to the monkey on the barstool beside him, as if either one might choose to answer.

'Panther?' Coley said. The question surprised him because the answer was so obvious he never thought anyone would think to ask it. 'Well, he's my best friend, Shamie.'

'Ah. Sure a best friend is like a good winter coat,' Shamie nodded. 'You can't put a price on companionship. Unless you're a hoor, of course.'

With that, he sauntered down the bar and left the man and monkey to their own company. As soon as his back was turned, Panther jumped behind the counter and upended a bottle of Jack Daniels over his mouth.

'Hey, bad monkey!' Coley shouted, but Panther wouldn't stop drinking.

When Shamie came back down the bar, he said,

'That's fifteen pound you owe me, Coley. Unless your friend here has money.'

Panther got sick in the back seat of the car on the way home. And again on the dinner table as Coley was about to serve toasted-banana sandwiches. By the time Coley called the vet, Panther was shivering like something inside him was trying to get out. The vet arrived when it was dark, and as his car came up the driveway, the headlights lit up the inside of the kitchen and swept over Panther lying prone on the table. Coley watched the white light play over the monkey and pass through his ears like he was made of paper.

'Help is here, little fella,' he said, and used a damp cloth to clean the drool from Panther's chin.

At the front door, the vet stooped to enter and, once inside, removed his wide-brimmed hat exposing an unloved crop of grey hair. Without saying a word to Coley, he sat down opposite Panther and lifted the hood of his eyelids – shining a pen-light into his blood-shot eyes. Panther moaned and struggled to move, but hadn't the energy, and slumped back down onto the kitchen table.

'Will he be alright, doctor?'

'He has alcohol poisoning. He'll most likely live, but I can't stress enough how dangerous it is to give hard liquor to a small animal.'

'It wasn't *my* idea or anything. He's a demon for the drink. Ask anyone.'

'Coley, you are his guardian. You have to understand that you are responsible for everything he does.'

'I see.'

'Do you though? You *cannot* allow him drink anymore.'

'Fair enough, doc. I'll have a word with him.'

Coley made Panther stick to the porter from then on.

'No more spirits,' he told him.

But it didn't do any good. Tourists, barmen, curious old women in headscarves – they all wanted to see the monkey drink a shot of whiskey. It soon became common knowledge around the village of Boyle that Panther was liable to do anything when he had a drop of liquor in him. At first, people knocked great sport out of watching him wrap his two little hands around a shot glass, then put his dukes up when he tried to pick a fight, but the novelty of that soon wore out.

They weren't welcome in Hughes's Pub anymore, but Sweeney's was the place to be after Friday night bingo anyway. Coley addressed the pub as he entered, booming a warm,

'How ye all!'

Panther imitated him by screeching loud enough to rend the atmosphere. At the bar, a trio of gummy farmers with their flat caps and hairy ears didn't even turn around to acknowledge them. In the lounge by the fireplace, a knot of string-lipped women with their tightly-wound perms ignored them too. Only Podge Sweeney, the barman, returned their greeting with a thumbs-up. Coley ordered a pint and a shot glass of lager, and the two sat down at the far end of the bar.

'He's very excitable. I think he upset the auld wans with that racket.'

'Yeah, sorry about that, Podge. He sometimes gets this way when he's hungry. Give us over three packets of peanuts there, it might quieten him down a bit. One salted for me and two dry roasted for himself.'

'Well aren't ya a little savage for the dry roasted.' Podge said, leaning his elbows on the counter to look Panther in the eye. 'Aren't ya?'

Panther stared back at Podge over the rim of his shot glass. The man had a short-bristled white goatee and a glass eye that skewed to the left and gave the illusion of a wide field of vision.

'So, what can he do, Coley?'

'Everything. He could drive a car if you had one that fit the size of him.'

'Can he laugh, like?'

'Only if you tickle him. He doesn't really get jokes.'

Coley was still trying to open the foil wrapper of peanuts with his teeth when Podge put his hand out to tickle Panther. Seeing the pudgy fingers reach for him, the monkey scampered under Coley's arm and tugged on his sleeve.

'Ah Jesus, settle, would ya. We only got here.'

Coley tried the packet of peanuts once more and ripped it in two, scattering nuts on the bar and the floor.

'Fuckin' look what ya made me do! Behave yourself, now, Panther. I mean it. Just fuckin' lay off.'

Coley shook his head and pushed Panther out from under his arm towards Podge who took him up in his hands and began to tickle him. The monkey was squirming and his face was getting redder, like you'd sometimes see a baby do before you had to change its nappy. Coley knew how to read these warning signs, and got as far as saying,

'Eh, Podge, I think he might need to—'

But it was too late and Panther had already released a curling stool on to the bar. Podge Sweeney wouldn't have them in his bar after that.

A man from the ISPCA called the following week to see how Panther was enjoying living with Coley.

'So, Coley,' he said, his grand Dublin accent piping out his nose. He had a full beard and a bushy head of hair that gave him a leonine look, and made Coley wonder about the man's parents. 'What do you feed Panther apart from bananas?'

They were in the back yard surrounded by towers of empty Fyffes crates which Coley had been meaning to burn. The question seemed to be an accusation of some sort.

'Nothing else. I'll swear to that.' Coley said, rubbing the back of his neck with his good hand.

Coley learned from the hairy Dubliner that monkeys ate much more than just bananas. This, despite all evidence from The Jungle Book, or Tarzan, or those films with Clint

Eastwood and the Orang-utan. However, even worse than being shown up by a townie, Coley was put out by how much a balanced diet for Panther was going to cost. The insurance money which he expected to last ten years of steady drunkenness would be all but gone in the next year if Panther didn't slow down. His appetite for bananas and whiskey was running Coley into the ground.

Panther, of course, had his own frustrations with the relationship. He was born into the circus and was used to being surrounded by men and women of talent; acrobats, and strongmen who could rip telephone books in two. Coley could barely read the telephone book. Sometimes he fell down on his way home from the pub but it wasn't funny like when the clowns did it in the big tent.

However, it wasn't Coley's ten-watt personality that rankled Panther the most – it was his thumb. That damned crippled thumb always pointing up, or out, or down, depending on which way Coley's arm was set. Even when he couldn't see it, the fact that he knew it was there pointing to somewhere was like a grain of sand in his eye, slowly aggravating him more and more to the point where Panther could think of nothing else but of cutting it off and burying it in the ground as deep as he could.

Of course, running away was another obvious solution, but as if Coley had expected this, he bought Panther a collar and leash and rarely left him unattended without either putting him in his cage or tying the leash to a post with a strong knot.

Then, one Tuesday afternoon in Daly's pub, Panther got his chance to escape. The pair had come in for a bite to eat before the main course of pints. Bruno Daly, the barman, placed a bowl of soup and a toasted sandwich on the bar.

'A solid breakfast beats two dinners in a row,' he said.

Coley reached across and took the soup in the same hand that he held Panther's leash. Panther, seeing his opportunity, ran around the back of Coley's legs and pulled on the leash, knocking the hot soup all over his master's belly.

'Jesus wept!' he screamed, and dropped the leash.

The front door was closed, so Panther ran up the chimney, where no one could get to him.

Coley tried to lure him with a banana, then tried it with whiskey, then with both. He stayed there all afternoon wafting a Chiquita Junior and a double Jameson in the hearth, hoping that Panther would come back down.

'He'll have to sometime,' Bruno said, 'there's a wire mesh in the chimney pot to stop the crows building nests, so he can't escape out the top.'

Word spread throughout the village, and soon people were coming in off the street to watch. Coley turned from the fireplace to see a gallery of faces. Beady-eyed Sergeant Curley was there. Father Gantley too, with his camera. Of course, all the gossip-mongers from Moran's shop had made it their business to get front row seats. A line of them sat there staring, each of them clutching varying shades of brown leatherette hands bags and a hot port.

'I suppose this is a grand bit of entertainment for ye?' Coley said. 'Have ye come to see my friend get killed?'

After lunchtime had passed with no sign of breaching the stand-off, Bruno suggested they smoke him out.

'He'll just get a little dizzy and fall right down.'

'On to a fire,' Coley noted.

Bruno had not quite thought that far ahead. 'Maybe just a little one, then?'

'No. We'll call the fire brigade.' Coley said. 'They'll be able to fetch him out.'

'Sure I suppose, what's the difference really between a cat stuck up a tree and a monkey stuck up a chimney?'

Bruno had meant to lighten the mood with that comment, but Coley just blinked at the black fireplace and said, 'Yeah. I suppose so.'

A fire truck arrived shortly after and beeped its way through the tangle of onlookers outside Bruno's pub. A fireman climbed the ladder reaching onto the roof and, removing the wire mesh, ran a hose into the chimney pot. He signalled to the fire truck below and water blasted through. Almost instantly, Panther came down into the grate with a flood of water. Coley had placed several pillows there so Panther bounced when he landed, wet and shivering. His hair was black from the soot and his eyes shone like glinting daggers. There was rolling applause from the gapers, and a fresh rush to the bar.

'Look at you,' Coley said. He held Panther tightly in a red tartan blanket. 'Your jacket's completely ruined.'

Coley put Panther in his cage and set it in the front passenger seat. Then he slammed down the wing of the Delorean. The wheels threw up gravel as they took off, and when they were out of town Coley punched the steering wheel with the one hand he could make into a fist.

'You made a prime fuckin' eegit out of me today. Is it not enough that you have to drink all me money, but now you have to embarrass me in front of the whole town as well? Look at me. I'm talking to you.'

But Panther wouldn't look at him. He spent the entire journey staring out the passenger window at the green tree-tops rushing by. His tiny fingers clutched the bars of the cage.

The following day, Coley received a letter from the fire station. It stated in formal legalese, which he found hard to follow, that he owed them £500 for 'rescuing' Panther.

Coley went for a walk. He did not stop to talk to his neighbours where he saw them working in their gardens. He took the curved road into the woods, and stayed there for most of the day throwing stones at fish in the stream, and smashing dead branches off moss-covered tree trucks.

When he came back to the house it was early evening and the midges were starting to gather and swarm. Panther's cage was set on a blue painted table on the back porch. Coley came through the back door and set a kerosene lamp down beside the cage. He was wearing a long wax coat. From one pocket he removed two shot glasses and lay them down on the peeling blue surface of the table. He took a bottle of Jack Daniels out of his other coat pocket and set it down with the label facing into the cage.

'Your favourite,' he said.

But the monkey still refused look at him. He hadn't made a sound or eaten anything since his attempt to escape.

'Panther, we have to talk,' he said, and put his hands on either side of the cage.

The next day when he came into Lawlor's alone, Moxy Lawlor asked, 'Where's your little companion, Coley?'

'I kilt the hoor,' Coley said, waiting for his Guinness to settle.

Moxy watched him stare into the cascading particles of dark and light, his eyes glazed over and raw-rimmed. Moxy had counselled many broken hearts at his bar and recognised the symptoms.

'Sure, there's plenty more fish in the sea, Coley.'

'Ah go fuck yourself, Moxy. It was a monkey, not a fish.'

And that was the last thing anyone in Boyle ever heard Coley Maguire say. After that he disappeared. His father's house was sold, and rumour filtered through the real estate agent that the money was routed to a small village near Mbandaka, in the Democratic Republic of Congo.

Wood Chopper

by Trish Holmes

He was an electrician by trade, but his passion was chopping wood. I had travelled far from my northern home as he had from his in the red Outback, and we found each other in the grey stone hostel underneath Edinburgh's mammoth castle.

Chiselled valleys and stiff peaks of ridged muscle were among the many benefits of wood-chopping. I imagined my life with him as an imported wife while he, the father of my children, stood on top of the wood-chopping medal podium. Then a friend let slip that the Wood Chopper was also sleeping with a short blonde from New Zealand.

I decided to get even.

Tears fell from his big blue eyes and eventually he offered two hundred pounds for the procedure. He said he couldn't stay with me. His feelings were stronger for the New Zealander and his social life was finally improving. Within hours word had spread, a development I hadn't anticipated. Jen Smith told me she was on my side and offered support. We walked to the hospital together and then she hugged me and left after I insisted on going on ahead by myself. I lingered in a ward full of old people in wheelchairs and watched her leave through a large window. Afterwards I walked over to St Andrew's Square and spent some of the money on a silk scarf that was orange.

I saw the Wood Chopper for the last time in the pub a few nights later. He and the New Zealander were arguing. Rumour was they were having difficulties. I never told him what happened to his baby. In fact, he never asked.

Carton Press

by Paul McMahon

Carton Press – otherwise known as Odd Ball – was born on April 17th, 1970, at twenty-four minutes past twelve on a sunny afternoon in the Mater Hospital in the centre of Belfast. At precisely that same moment, in the west of the city, Carton's father came home for lunch. He remembered, he told Carton years later, looking at his watch as he took the door keys out of his pocket, being amazed and annoyed at how such a short walk from the house where he was fixing a roof could take almost twenty five minutes. Then the phone rang. Carton came a day early.

When Carton was one year old his hair was blond. When he started school he was five years old and his hair was dark brown. He ran away from home for the first time when he was six. Well, he hid in the dog kennel in the back yard, staying there until it got dark. Rebel, the hardy mongrel sheepdog that was given to the Press family by the coalman the year before, sat beside him and they both watched the anxious scurrying of feet going past the kennel door. When hunger finally got the upper hand and little Carton got out of the kennel and walked in the back door, the baffled posse in the kitchen fell silent. His mother smiled awkwardly at him and said she had a few friends over.

'Do you want some dinner?' Carton nodded his head and stared at the floor as usual. 'You can eat watching the TV if you want,' she said.

They never could have guessed as they scoured high and low along the length and breadth of the Andersonstown Road, that Carton was just a few feet away from the back door. They never guessed why he wanted to run away or why he continued to do so, or why one day he never came back.

On April 17th 1976, at approximately eight a.m., Mr Press went to wake Carton for school with seven lit candles flickering on a chocolate cake; he found his bed empty. It had become such a regular occurrence by this time that his father merely guffawed and went off to work. It was the same routine each time: Carton disappeared then returned in the afternoon with a wild excuse. Once he said he was shot by a rubber bullet and even showed a bruise on his thigh in his effort to prove it. Another time he said he was abducted by hoods

I was working with Press Senior that day. He came into work as usual. He didn't mention anything about Carton running away nor had he ever. We both had a cup of tea then went up onto the roof. The semi-derelict building was on a hill and we had a panoramic view of the Black Mountain and the roof tops of the estates as they stretched towards the city centre, four kilometres away. Smoke was rising from a burning bus on the Andersonstown Road. I think a car was burning also. I remembered getting into my own car that morning with a sigh of relief that it hadn't been stolen as it was my turn to go for timber supplies. They used stolen cars to fortify the barricades, I didn't mention anything to Press that my own son Ciarán, was not in his bed that morning. Or that I had found pages and pages of scribbled writings on his desk. On one of his scribbled pages I deciphered an account of a Christ-like vision; it spoke of a mystical experience, the force in all things, the death and rejuvenation of the world. It described a bird of flames in the sky, the ground coming alight and spreading outwards like a wave of flame. It detailed crawling through undergrowth, the scents of dry leaves, mosses, damp bark, running water, the bellowing of petroleum, the whirr of engines and the illuminated skyline at night above the houses.

Press seemed a little detached that morning. We weren't under any time pressure. Maybe he was just daydreaming, I thought to myself at the time. The sky was blue and the forecast for the coming week promised an unprecedented spell of dry weather. It was at about eleven a.m. that Press positioned a nail against a rafter with his right hand – he was left-handed – and, after raising the hammer in an arc, brought it down sharply onto the flat head of the nail in perfect synchronicity with a car-bomb that detonated somewhere in the city centre. We both crouched close to the rafters, then after deep breaths, looked towards the city. Press picked up another nail, held it point first against the wooden beam and looked at me with a glint in his eye.

'Go on,' I taunted him, 'I dare ye'.

At one p.m. Press and myself went to a café across from St Agnes' Church for lunch. As soon as we sat down at the window an old pensioner whispered to us, pointing to the new phone kiosk which had suddenly replaced the previous one which was burnt-out the week before by local hoods.

'Aye, did ye hear? Anyone damages the phone box again gets a six pack. They start burning one thing for a cause and then other people get carried away and start burning anything just for the fun of it. I got a look at them that burnt it. The boys'll get them.'

A six pack is the street term for being shot in both ankles, both knees and both elbows, a punishment shooting. It would be administered by 'the boys', the IRA.

'Ah, thanks for tellin' us,' said Press, 'I was just gonna burn it on the way back to work, jus' for the craic.'

The pensioner wasn't in the mood for Press' humour and turned back to the cold tea with tight eyes narrowed towards the kiosk. With hindsight I know that Press was preoccupied that day with Carton. I still hadn't tied the two together, Carton and my own son Ciarán.

When I went home that evening, my wife told me that Ciarán was in his room. I stood outside his bedroom door for a moment before going in. Carton was there too. They were talking in whispers. When I opened the door they looked up at me in surprise.

'Ciarán, your dinner is ready soon,' I said to him, as a preamble to the ear warming I was planning to give him as soon as Carton left.

'Hello, Mr Byrne,' said Carton, standing up to shake my hand. 'My Da said he set off a car-bomb in the city today and that you told him to do it.'

I smiled then nodded at Ciarán before going back downstairs. The accusation had me reeling for the rest of the evening. Carton had changed dramatically but I couldn't put my finger on just how. He was called Odd Ball behind his back because he had two different coloured eyes — one was blue and one was brown. They both shone brilliantly.

I drank a crate of beer and staggered off to bed. Next morning Ciarán was gone again. I found more pages of scribbles on his desk. The Christ-like visions were again recounted, more illuminations, huge burnings on the road, a dawn of fire, kiosks of flames; it seemed to be fragments torn from the journal of a drugged poet writing in the dark. I stuffed the pages into my pocket.

Press was on the roof, pulling back the plastic covering, as I pulled up outside the house. It was April, the 18th. The pensioner from the café was walking towards me with the sun rising in the background.

'So, this is where you're workin', is it?' Said the pensioner.

'Well, did anyone burn it yet?' Press shouted down.

'Not yet, but I'll be the first one to call the boys if I see anything,' the old crone snapped back. She was probably on her way back to the café to billet the telephone kiosk.

'Just as well I put that plastic covering over the roof, eh?' Press said to me as I climbed up onto the roof. 'If I ever see that forecaster I'll give him a fuckin' eight-pack.'

'It should hold off for the day though,' I said.

When I got up onto the roof, Press was sitting on a cross-beam, smoking a roll-up and looking towards the Black Mountains.

'It should be called Shaved Hill,' he said. 'People call anything a mountain in this country. Look at it,' he went on, shaking his head in contempt at Black Mountain, 'that is a hill. Not a fuckin' tree or even a bush on it. You can see everything.'

'There are all sorts of places to hide up there. You just can't see them — that's what makes them such good hiding places. Did you know your Da when you were a kid?' I asked.

'Nobody knew their Das in those days.'

'But did you want to get to know him?'

'Aye, I wanted to get t'know him all right but he hadn't the least conception as to how to communicate with kids.'

'It was the same with me, exactly. I think, for our generation, there's been some kind of reversal. We wanted to get to know our Das when we were kids but they couldn't communicate with us. And now that we want to get to know our kids they've no interest in us.'

For a few minutes the sky looked like it might rain then it turned blue again. Twenty minutes later we pulled the plastic covering over the bare rafters and sat looking down along the street. There was smoke rising from the Andersonstown

Road next to the steeple of St Agnes' church, a long black tail rising up into the sky. The sky was closed-in as though it was hovering just overhead. The sky over the Andersonstown Road always looked close. It seemed to start at the top of the shaved hill of Black Mountain and then stretch tightly over just above the roof tops. What good would it do, I was thinking to myself, to read Ciarán's scribbles to Press?

'It's all a lack of communication. Nobody knows … anything,' said Press.

Carton and Ciarán ran across the street no more than one hundred yards away from where we sat on the roof. They had appeared out of an alleyway that leads onto a car-park beside St Agnes' Church. Moving away from us they ran along the pavement, turned the bend, disappeared, and never returned.

María Magdalena

by Alan Caden

Michael once beat a man to death in Riga. The man had accidentally let slip a mooring-rope that whipped across Michael's face. It left a raw diagonal furrow from brow to cheek of a face that was not, even before that accident, a teenage girl's dream. When he got out of prison, he discovered a son he had never known. The mother was now a junkie. Cheap heroin from Kaliningrad was flooding the streets of a newly-free Baltic. He doesn't know now if she is dead, or if she is a slave in a room in some European city. He doesn't care, or pretends not to. He loves only that child, who lives with Michael's mother. Michael looms in the doorways and gangways, his gargantuan frame blocking the light for a few moments and then moving on, working quietly. He works twice as hard as any of the others, though none of them, save Xi Liao, could be called slackers. Michael speaks little and seldom repeats himself.

He is holding a long Bowie knife he bought in Gdansk.

'Bastard. I talking to you.'

Captain Blanco looks him up and down with contempt then puts out his cigarette.

'Loo', I already say you *cabrones* – fuck off! I have wor' to do and so do you.'

The *María Magdalena* is a ghost ship, a boat with an origin at least as obscure as those of her crewmen. Built in Taipei (according to its records), registered in Panama (according to its owner) and plying its trade only from the Baltic across the North Sea (according to its captain). Only the bare necessities work aboard the vessel, and this vital machinery is well maintained by Xi Liao, the chief engineer. The Captain has the boat painted a jolly red twice a year and the name is written in a curling script, like a boat from children's TV. He knows this decoration is more than worth the money. Everything else – toilets, galley, mess, sleeping quarters – is falling apart, rusted and unloved. The *María* is a workhorse, a mule of the sea that carries the hopes of its crew, though not one of them has spent a pleasant moment on board. Not one of them feels anything for it but a bitter, grudging respect that she does not buck and spill them into the freezing water. But the *María* has a large hold and fills it more often than not, while the other ships complain that all the stocks have disappeared.

'Bastard! We go to Custom now. We tell them,' Michael states.

The Captain ignores him. He studies the charts.

Captain Blanco is a bastard. Every crewman who has ever served under him has called him 'Bastard', each in their own tongue. He demands much, gives little and does not tolerate errors. They say he has thrown men into the North Sea for disrespect. Yet he fills the nets with fish and that fills the bank accounts of the men who despise him. His sallow, jaundiced skin and sad eyes hide a sadistic streak. Any man who gets between him and his work incurs a cold tide of vengeance known from A Coruña to Stávanger. The only man Blanco defers to is a mysterious Russian named Stolypin, who Blanco maintains is the owner of the boat. He talks regularly with this Russian on his mobile phone, but observes a fanatic secrecy in these calls so that none of the crew have ever seen or heard this man who holds their destinies in his hands.

The *María* holds six crew.

'What's happening? What does he say? We get paid or what?' Says one of the other crewmen, jostling forward a step or two.

'Ssshh, shuya fugn mout an geback! Migal he toggin to Bassid now, lemme lissenin,' responds Xi Liao. He pushes backwards against the other man, so that his slight frame remains out of Blanco's sight. He has seen the Captain's anger.

Only he knows that Captain Blanco has a young lover whom he dotes upon, a dusky Portuguese beauty who the boat is named after. She is the bottomless well of youth and frippery where the Captain's substantial wages disappear. Someday, she says, she will marry him, but for now she is too young. Around this young woman, The Bastard is a pussycat, a fawning sugar-daddy who indulges her every whim. He speaks softly to her of his feelings and makes extravagant declarations in perfumed love poems he plagiarises from Darío and Neruda. Were he to admit it to himself, she could do to him what no storm or swell, no reef or Customs, no man or moment has ever done – break him.

Captain Blanco, the Galician, holds a gun that his father gave him, a gun once used to shoot Republicans in the back of the head. His fingers curl around the butt, where the criss-cross grip has worn smooth. One eye takes in Michael's huge form.

'You listen me, Bastard? We not work. We not unload until we get money. Fish will go bad.'

Michael knows better than to appeal to Blanco's humanity, to explain that these men have families, mortgages, debts above their heads. Fish and money, that is all that matters.

'Ya, Blanno, innashnal law. Where u fugn Rushn now, hah?' Xi Liao pipes up.

Xi Liao is a spiteful and mischievous spirit of the under-decks. He claims to be Taiwanese not Chinese, though none of the others care. In his alternative pasts, he was a protester at Tianamen Square, a miner in the Gobi desert, a hurricane chaser, a China Sea pirate, a Taiwanese secret agent or the son of a murdered millionaire. He talks without cease, keeping time with his engine, but he has long since stopped speaking his native language and has adopted a cant of the sea, a tongue sounding like English, but with few recognisable rules or sounds. He is lazy and indolent, but he can caress the capricious engine with such tenderness that it purrs beneath his, and only his, touch. None of the crew know what he does with his money but they presume that, like many of the Chinese sailors, his vice is gambling. Xi Liao's hand is poised on a mobile phone in his hoodie pocket. The Port Authority number is on the screen.

The Captain turns his gaze to his cigarette case, ignoring the assembly. He puts a Ducado to his lips and lights it, all with his left hand, and goes back to perusing the charts. None of these men finds silence uncomfortable.

'Bastard! I say we go to Custom now.'

'No, you Leethuanian fuck. You no going nowhere,' Blanco says.

'I Latvian,' Michael's voice rises, menacing. 'And yes, we go. You want stop me?'

The other three crew-men stand unmoving on the deck, their heads uncovered to the drizzle that sheets languidly across Dublin Bay like the thin hairs on an old grey dog. There is a last crane still working, unloading a Maersk Sealand container of Irish flags for Saint Patrick's Day, stitched with care in Taipei. On one side, the crew can see the lights of the IFSC, Dublin's attempt at a high-rise financial district. On the other, they can barely make out the dull, low shape of Bull Island through Dublin Port's lights. A sea-wall built by Captain William Bligh in a later incarnation, it stretches out to an automated lighthouse and a statue of the Virgin Mary – Stella Maris. They do not know this city, the

Captain never lets his crew into port. They stand squarely, their nervous eyes narrowed and set on Michael's broad shoulders and beyond, to the seated figure of their Captain. One of them holds a slash-hook loosely in his hand. The rain on the cracked frosted windows of the cabin blurs the array of lamps and lights from outside, turning the basic wheelhouse into a hallucinogenic light show of blues and reds and sea-greens, a multi-coloured Neptune's Cave. The red shifts across Michael's face, and Blanco imagines he can see the knot and weft of the rope that changed his life. Behind him, Xi Liao is lurking, peering out from under alternate arms like a curious hyena.

Michael flexes the fingers of his free hand. In the Middle Ages, men like him would have crushed babies' heads in their hands, would have lifted knights in full armour from their horses with a single stroke of an axe. Blanco takes a long drag on the black tobacco and considers Michael's challenge. Men like Blanco were wrecked on the Irish coast in the Spanish Armada and made their way home. Men like him subdued, murdered and raped their way through the New World in search of gold. As he speaks, the acrid smoke of the black tobacco coils to form part of the light-show. The boat bobs gently against the dock as the tide rises.

'Hah! I stop you, no problems ...Leesten me, my friend. One time. Get the fuck off my breedge, I tell you now. Go, have a wank yoursel', or theenk about your precious son. Or both. I don' care. Just fuck off. All of you assholes.'

He points the cigarette at each in turn, names them. Fear is an unprofitable emotion for Captain Blanco, something for which there is no place in the ship's log. He has calmly thrown fish overboard while under bombardment from the Icelandic navy, spat in their faces when they boarded the ship and then got off on a technicality. He has faced down murderers and pirates. He has laughed at jittery 17-year olds on military service as they asked for bribes. He thinks of María, blinks hard and spits. He slowly extends his hand toward Michael and without looking, raises his yellow-stained middle finger, the cigarette smoking between his thumb and index finger.

'Let thees sheet go, Miguel, las' chance. Or you can as' the devil for another job.'

'OK. So you pay us. *Then* we fuck off.' Michael puts out his palm.

'Ya Blano you bastidy bassid you pay fugn money or you no li whas gon appen mufuga.'

'I don' got no money to pay you, like I tell you before, so you shut up and make the work. You weel get your fucking money but don' bother me no more. An' remember – the bullet don' care how big you are, you Latvian *hijoputa*.'

Michael does not move but grips his hand tight around the handle of his knife. For one whole evening last year, while his son was sick, he wound monofilament net twine around the handle. His hand will not slip. Both of these men come from a time of military service, from a time of dictatorships and harsh judgements. They know this about each other. Once started, one of them will have to die. Michael thinks of his son, who knows things like equations and what happened in history. Michael knows none of these things. He tries to clear his mind of the paralysing fear of what will become of his son if Blanco shoots him. Rent is overdue. Michael's mother will not live much longer.

Captain Blanco leans his elbow against the desk where the log-book lies open, ready to be inspected by Irish customs. The Captain's writing is neat, with big friendly loops that belie the murderous thoughts in his mind. He thinks of his lover and wonders what she would do without him. He knows the answer, but refuses to accept it. Every man needs something on the sea.

'Fastnet Rock. Wind Force 2. Falling slightly. Lambay Island. Wind Force 3. Gusts rising to Force 4 or 5. Carnsore Point …'

Both of the men cock their ears and listen to the report. Muscles loosen slightly. Each keeps their eyes on the other but in their heads they are flying, following the progress of the winds and tides from North to South along the east coast of this island. Outside on deck, some of the crew turn to look as a two young Chinese women pass by, on their way home after ten hours gutting fish. One of them glances moon-faced at the scene on the deck of the *Maria*. She checks her stride for a moment, sensing that something is wrong, then keeps walking. This is none of her business. She has a work visa. In her pocket are her wages for a forty-hour week. It is more than any of the crew get for their seventy-hour week, and a lot more than nothing.

The weather report moves onto the west coast, wild waters that many of these men have fished, but the Atlantic does not concern them now.

'Bastard. Is too long. You fuck with us. You think I am fool, yes?'

'I say what happen on my fucking boat, abortion. Don' poosh it. The money it will come.'

Blanco switches off the radio and turns his back on the crew, busying himself with the cosmetic surgery of the log-book details. A tug boat is guiding in a big tanker, loaded with oil and God knows what. Blanco boasts that he has never smuggled, not a thing. He is a fisherman, he says, not a pirate.

'Bastid, we fugn phone iland cussems …'

Blanco swivels around and levels the gun at Xi Liao, who tries to bob out of the line of sight of Blanco's baleful eyes, the infinite grey of the sea.

'You no' that fuckin stoopid, *chino*. You no call nobody. You know what happen.'

'No, Bastard, he mean we already call this. Before. We call them, tell them. They give us number. For union. We are not take this shit, Bastard. Three months you say money will come, money will come. I think you steal it. I think maybe you are thief,' Michael says.

Blanco nods slowly, three times, then raises his eyebrows at Michael and cocks the trigger.

'You fuckin stay here in Ireland with your union, Russian communist. Get tha fuck off my boat now or I will make your son a bastard too. Belee' me.'

Michael is not moving. The crew behind who cannot see step forward, craning their necks and forcing Michael to take a half a step forward. Xi Liao slinks back towards the gangway. He has seen bullets ricochet off the metal rooms of a ship, seen people killed by their own bullets. He has seen knives move quicker than trigger-fingers. He has seen small men murder giants. And he has seen all these things from the furthest distance possible. The crane has stopped unloading. The only sounds are the strenuous grind of a tug boat and the low growl of twisting screws somewhere, the bass travelling underwater and penetrating the senses of the men from up through the floor; it's a continuous throb they only notice when it is absent. The wind gusts up.

A sudden blur of dirty white; a high crack; a fissure shoots across the glass. There's a dull thud as a misguided sea-gull's body follows its beak headlong into the strengthened glass. Its blood and feathers splatter all over the windscreen, its bones smash into pieces that the other gulls will eat tomorrow.

A glint of steel.

A muzzle-flash.

Michael gazes at the window. He will ring his mother and she will pass the phone to his son, who will babble about his day at school and ask his father which kinds of fish he caught today. Michael will promise he'll be home soon. Blanco stares at Michael in disbelief. After, he will call María and ask her to marry him. He will not accept her refusal and they will set a date. He will tell her that he will leave the seas. Then he will be happy.

A Shoe Falls

by Colm Brady

Doherty decided to walk away from the world, to reach the horizon and walk right off the edge. When you are walking off the world you need a good pair of shoes. These were not the shoes he should have taken. These were his mass, interview and funeral shoes. They were thick-soled black leather with welted uppers. Over time the leather upper overhung the worn sole at the back. The leather was like the broad bow of a galleon as it carried the captain's stateroom over the boiling ocean, hanging there defiantly. The laces were the rounded variety he preferred but they were worn to a central thread. One good tug and he would be left late for mass or the funeral or the interview, holding half a frayed shoelace in one hand while the other hand made a fist in the air.

Doherty's trousers were navy with the tag still attached to the waist. He had a belt threaded through some of the loops and a shirt creased against the dawn light. He met a man on a bicycle on the main road. The man stared at the coatless Doherty – it was a cold morning.

'Hardy man.'

Doherty grunted in response. He decided to get off the main road and headed down a lane to the right. He walked on the green strip in the middle. His footsteps were silent and the grass gave under his feet with each step. The lane was climbing gradually and the tawny-coloured bogland was planted with trees. Firs and spruces that came right up to the edge of the lane, wretched trees stripped of their branches like cancerous fingers accusing the sky. The moss on the ground deadened every footfall; sound sucked out like a bell jar, but he could still see the horizon through the gap made by the lane. If he could reach that gap he would be free.

He saw a small red flash from his shirt pocket. The mobile phone showed the texts from before the journey.

'Where are you? I need the car. You are not to drive.'

He stared at the screen. The letters looked so final, so finished. He deleted the message. The screen said that he had seven missed calls from her. That had been when the match was on. Chicken nuggets and chips for the kids and a couple of pints for him.

'Can a man not have a quiet drink and get a bit of peace?'

Everyone at the bar looked at the television, the only ones who looked at him were the kids. They liked the orange and Tayto and old men with whiskey breath telling them how good they were. They knew this was a new pub though. He didn't want to go to the old places any more. Things had happened there, things they didn't want to remember. Shouting that they were thieving bastards and that all a man needed was a few pints and the companionship of his fellows.

The lane got steeper. The trees pressed closer and whispered to him of social workers and arrangements and rights. Always rights. How was a man supposed to navigate this world when everybody had rights? What about him? The horizon was approaching, he would soon step off. The trees released their grip on the lane and he powered through patches of mist. He was high enough to have a view of the country. He could see past county boundaries. The light was harsher here, it hummed around his eyes. He climbed over a fence at the base of the hill – the high point. He stopped for a minute and read the next message.

'*I swear I will call the Guards if you don't bring them back. You can do what you want then. Please.*'

How did she expect him to react to that? The crimson visor came down. He must have driven back but he couldn't remember. He knocked at the door. Polite. Even a little smile, the smile that got her to dance with him at the start. As she took the chain off the door to let the kids in, he kicked it. Hard. It threw her against the wall, broke teeth and bruised her dismissive face. Her nose sprayed blood on his shirt. It was still there, hardening and maroon now. The kids tried to get him off her, skinny arms more suited to delivering bedtime hugs than fighting for survival. That was when he decided it was time for a walk. He changed his trousers quickly and started.

The last half mile was surfaced and steep. He felt like the King of Leinster surveying a world unchanged from before the Christians came, with their rules and shame. The mast was held by steel hawsers which stopped the wind crashing it down into the bog. Each one was as thick as a man's arm but when he looked up they were like the string that held a kite down to earth. The red warning beacons glowed; he relaxed as he placed his foot on the base of the mast. His eyes were streaming in the wind. He saw more with each rung and felt party to the secrets of the world. If she could see him she would say he was crying. Not him.

In a transmission station on the East Coast a man threw a switch. A signal travelled from his control panel to a concrete substation at the base of the mast. The children waited dull-eyed in the house. Doherty felt the hum and climbed faster. He was nearly at the top. He had to reach it so he could be taken up, like the Assumption. He passed the top beacon and scrambled to the summit. He was in a cylindrical mesh cage with an open top, ready to ascend. Children's television started and the power flowed through him. He screamed like a child in a funfair until his larynx burned out. They found his warped shoes at the base of the mast. The soles had bubbled with the heat but the wear on the heels was still visible.